The Good,
The Bad
and
The Lukewarm

A RELEVANT APPROACH TO THE
SEVEN CHURCHES IN REVELATION

by

DENIS LYLE M.A.

AMBASSADOR

BELFAST ◆ **GREENVILLE**
NORTHERN IRELAND   SOUTH CAROLINA

The Good, The Bad and The Lukewarm

© Copyright 1997 Denis Lyle

ISBN 1 84030 014 0

AMBASSADOR PRODUCTIONS LTD,
Providence House
16 Hillview Avenue,
Belfast, BT5 6JR
Northern Ireland

Emerald House,
1 Chick Springs Road, Suite 206
Greenville,
South Carolina 29609
United States of America

Contents

❖

Foreword

❖

As overseer of the churches in Asia the Apostle John writes to seven of the churches, facing different problems and difficulties, to offer commendation, condemnation, counsel and encouragement. The problems faced by these churches are problems faced by churches down through the ages and are still faced by churches today. Hence the messages found in Revelation two and three are vitally important.

The author of this volume presents a careful study of the historical background of each of the seven churches, which will help the reader understand the origin of the problems which arose in the churches. He then examines the solution recommended by the Apostle John, to each of these specific problems. Encouragement is given to each church to show that their problems have a solution so their situation is not hopeless. Each letter concludes with an encouraging promise and an exhortation to respond to the correction the Apostle gives.

One can find examples of the problems the first century churches faced, in this twentieth century. The solutions to their problems will provide guidance for the solution of our problems today. Hence the material presented in this study is very practical as well as needed. The author uses many illustrations to make the truth clear. His application of the message to the churches is convicting, convincing and pointed. This work is highly recommended to all who are exercised to see that our churches conform to the pattern designed by the Great Head of the Church.

J. Dwight Pentecost
Distinguished Professor of Bible Exposition, emeritus
Dallas Theological Seminary

Preface

❖

Church life is never easy. It never was. Christians at the end of the first century did not find it easy, nor do we today. Joining a church can be like falling in love and getting married. Its terrific at first, but the glow of the honeymoon period begins to fade and reality sets in. You're married to another human being who, like you, has failings. How optimistic we are when we join a new church. It will be thrilling, we think, to work with a hundred other believers. But after a while things seem different, do they not?

The seven churches the Risen Lord examines in the book of Revelation are typical and representative of what every local church has been throughout her history and what she is like today. Any condition of any church in any place at any time may be found in these seven churches. It may be that you will see your church depicted here. Indeed every thoughtful believer will find himself mirrored here. God grant us ears to hear what the Spirit is saying to the churches.

This book is the outcome of a series of studies conducted at the 'Iron Hall', Belfast, on Monday evenings. During the series I drew widely from writers both old and new. Their writings inspired me and permeate this book. That is my disclaimer to plagiarism.

I am thankful to the Lord who blessed these studies when preached first to large and eager congregations. I am also grateful to God's people in the 'Iron Hall' who encourage me continually as I preach the Word. Finally, I greatly appreciate the constant support of my family.

Denis Lyle
Belfast 1997

Chapter One

A Very Special Book

❖

Someone has rightly observed that the Book of Genesis and the Book of Revelation are like two bookends that hold the entire Bible together. The parallels between these two books are many. For example, in the Book of Genesis, the first man Adam reigns on the earth. In Revelation, the last Man reigns in heaven in glory. In Genesis, the darkness and the sea's are created. In Revelation, there is no more darkness or any sea. In Genesis, a bride, Eve is presented to her husband. In Revelation, the church is presented to her husband, the Lord Jesus Christ. In the Book of Genesis we see the tree of life in the Garden of Eden. In the Book of Revelation, we see the tree of life in God's new creation. In Genesis we see the beginning of sin brings death and a curse. In Revelation, sin is done away with: there is no more curse and no more dying.

In Genesis, Satan appears to man for the first time. In Revelation he appears for the last time. In the book of Genesis, man is driven from the garden and from God's presence. In the book of Revelation, man sees God's face again in glory. In Genesis men look for a city by faith. In Revelation, the holy city is presented to men in glory. In Genesis Satan utters the first lie ever heard: " ye shall not surely die." (Gen 3:4) In Revelation, there is a city where liars will never enter. Now it's important to see the books of Genesis and Revelation in comparison and contrast with one another. What God began so long ago at the first creation, He will ultimately complete in His new creation.

The Book of Revelation offers the believer a dramatic overview of the end-times, from the Rapture of the Church to the very end of the age. The apostle John was called away from fishing by Jesus Christ, became His best friend, and watched the ministry of the Lord develop. He was there on the Mount of Transfiguration, in the Garden of Gethsemane, and at the foot of the cross of Calvary. Some of the last words Christ spoke in this world were to John, asking him to take care of Jesus' mother, Mary. John became a fearless preacher of the gospel, a leading evangelist and teacher in the early church and a holy writer of God's Word. He penned the fourth gospel, and three letters which he wrote to young believers and which are part of the holy canon of Scripture. Yet near the end of his life John was exiled to the barren island of Patmos by Domitian for preaching the truth of the Gospel. And while there John heard the voice of God calling him to heaven, where he was shown the events that would lead to the end of human history. John wrote the things that the angel told him to, and his book thus offers us instructive pictures of eventualities reaching on to the end of time.

(1) THE SPECIAL NATURE OF THE BOOK

J. Vernon McGee writes, " This book is like a great union station where the great trunk lines of prophecy come in from other portions of Scripture. Revelation does not originate, but consummates. It is imperative to a right understanding of the book to be able to trace each great subject of prophecy from the first reference to the terminal."

The first three verses of Revelation form a preface which tells us something about the purpose of the book: the importance of the book and the attitude in which this book is to be read. There are also some words in this opening paragraph that reveal to us the special nature of this book:

(a) MYSTERIES ARE EXPLAINED:

The Greek word which is translated " revelation," is apokalupsis which literally means " an unveiling." A revelation removes the veil which obscures our understanding, it unravels the mystery, it makes the meaning plain. Some years ago the city of Chicago was given an original by Pablo Picasso to adorn the plaza outside the new city hall. For months, as the statue was being erected, it was heavily screened from the curious gaze of the passers-by. When it was finished it stood in the plaza thickly veiled. The day came, however, when the Mayor of the city unveiled the statue to the astonished gaze of Chicago and the world. There it stood in all its glory,the latest offering at the altar of art, Chicago's own gigantic Picasso. Now what the Mayor did for Chicago when he unveiled the statue, the book of Revelation does for us. It draws aside the veil. As we move through the book of Revelation, we will find many mysteries made clear. Here there is set before us God's impending purposes for both the human race and the planet on which we live.

(b) PROPHECIES ARE ENCOUNTERED:

The other word used to describe the book of Revelation is " prophecy." (1:3) The Revelation is a book of prophecy. Seven times the noun " prophecy," (propheteia) appears (1:3 11:6 19:10 22:7,10,18,19) This is a book that deals in predictions. It deals with people and events which lie in the future. Powerful personalities are waiting to make their entrance on the stage of human events. Extraordinary circumstances are waiting to unfold as the juggernaut of history rumbles toward its consummation. We shall meet these personalities and witness these events in the book of Revelation. Of course the grand consummation of all prophecy is the coming again of Jesus Christ.

Seven times it is stated in this book that He will come. (1:7 2:25 3:3 3:11 22:7, 12, 20) So then this book is all about His Coming. The first time He came as Saviour: but the next time He will come as Sovereign. The first time He came humbly, and died on a cross as a suffering servant. Even though the OT prophets foretold the birth of the King, most people on earth missed it. But when Christ comes back no one will be able to miss it. He will return in power, and in glory and in majesty. He will defeat Satan and his armies, wipe sin from the face of the earth and set up His eternal kingdom.

(c) SYMBOLS ARE EMPLOYED:

The word signified (semaino) is interesting. If you want to get the true sense of this word pronounce it aloud: SIGN-I-FIED ! In other words Christ made His revelation known to John by signs or symbols and once you grasp the symbolic "significance," of this book, you can begin to understand and apply the book of Revelation. Revelation is a book of symbols and these symbols are important. Some symbols are explained. Lamps for example represent assemblies of God's people: stars represent angels: incense represent the prayers of saints. Other symbols are understood from OT symbolism (Rev 2:7 17: 4:7) and some symbols are not explained at all. (the white stone in 2:17)

Now because of the symbolic nature of Revelation, questions arise as to whether certain parts of it are to be understood symbolically or literally. A proper understanding of the book of Revelation requires both. For example (Rev

12:3-4) describes Satan as a great red dragon having a tail that could sweep one third of the stars out of heaven. Now that is obviously a symbolic description but it does not mean that Satan himself is not a literal being. The characterization of Satan as a dragon shows his ferocity and power. The stars represent angels that chose to follow him and fell from heaven. Now this is a symbolic representation of Satan, but it is to be believed quite literally.

(2) THE AUTHOR OF THE BOOK

Who is the author of the book of Revelation? (1:1) This book had its origin not in the mind of John, but in the mind of God. But how did the Lord convey the contents of this book to his servant John ? The Father gave the revelation to the Son (Matt 24:36) and the Son shared it with the apostle using "His angel," as intermediary. Now sometimes Christ Himself conveyed information to John (1:10) sometimes it was an elder (7:13) and often it was an angel. (17:1 19:9-10) Sometimes a " voice from heaven," told John what to say and do. (10:4) The book came from God to John no matter what the various means of communication were, and it was all inspired by the Holy Spirit. (2 Tim 3:16)

It's interesting to notice that the Holy Spirit used John to give us three kinds of inspired literature: the gospel of John: the three epistles: and the book of Revelation. These five books are in three main groups.

(a) THE GOSPEL: OUR PAST

The gospel of John has to do with our PAST and deals with the theme of salvation.

(b) THE EPISTLES: OUR PRESENT

The three epistles have to do with our present and deal with the theme of sanctification or daily growth in the Christian life.

(c) THE REVELATION: OUR FUTURE

The book that points to the future, to that glorious time when we shall see Him. The GOSPEL tells us TO BELIEVE: (John 20:31) The EPISTLES tell us to BE SURE: (1 John 5:13) and the Revelation tells us to BE READY: (22:20) But who is this man John, whose pen has preserved for us this awesome and powerful vision of the future ? In (1:4) he simply identifies himself as John, in (1:9) he describes his circumstances.

(1) GEOGRAPHICALLY:

Patmos. A rugged volcanic island off the coast of Asia Minor, about 10 miles long and 6 miles wide, located just off the coast of Turkey. Patmos was a penal colony settled by the Romans. It was the Alcatraz of the day. Like being shipped to Siberia for the winter. It was a remote place for exile for serious criminals against the Empire.

(2) CIRCUMSTANTIALLY:

" For the Word of God .... " (1:9) He was exiled there from AD 86-96. Probably put there by the Roman Emperor Domitian. John was labouring in the mines and quarries of Patmos. Busting rocks on a chain gang. Ninety years old. Separated from believers. Suffering persecution. Aged and forgotten. Confined. Without sufficient food. Improperly dressed. Sleeping on the bare ground of a dark cave. Cold. Lonely. Under the severe lash of an overseer. Imprisoned for preaching the gospel of Jesus Christ. It was Domitian who instigated emperor worship. It became law that no Christian would escape punishment who failed to worship Caesar and to renounce his allegiance to Christ. When John was brought before the tribunal he would not deny his Lord. The result ? Patmos.

It's when we are suffering and forgotten that God often unexpectedly breaks into our lives to use us in the greatest ways. This was true of John. And it is often true for us. John thought that his life and long ministry were over, but his most significant ministry was still before him. It was when the hour was darkest when the church was suffering and was seemingly defeated that Christ broke into John's life ! So that the Patmos of persecution became to John the open door for service.

(3) THE ORIGINAL READERS OF THE BOOK

The book is addressed in (1:4) "to the seven churches which are in Asia."

(a) THE PEOPLE THAT ARE IDENTIFIED:

Paul had sent letters to seven churches .... Rome, Corinth, Galatia, Ephesus, Philippi, Colossae and Thessalonica and now John sent one book to seven different churches. Upon arrival in Ephesus, the messenger would present the scroll to the leadership of the church and they would read it publicly to the congregation. (1:3) A copy would then be made before the other messengers would depart with the original document to the next city. (22:18-19) Thus, all seven churches received the entire book of Revelation. Why were these seven churches singled out by the Lord? Certainly there were more than seven churches in the area. (Col 1:2 4:13 Acts 20:5) But the spiritual conditions found in these seven are typical and representative of what every local church has been throughout her history and what she is like today.

(b) THE PROMISE THAT IS SPECIFIED:

" Blessed is he that readeth and they that hear the words of this prophecy." (1:3) No book in the Bible has an introduction and a conclusion quite like this one. It commences with a promised blessing and it closes with a promised blessing. (22:7) Indeed there are seven beatitudes in this book, all

beginning with the word " blessed." (1:3 14:13 16:15 19:9
20:6 22:7 22:14) Now the blessing here relates to those who
HEAR what the book has to say and to those who HEED what
the book has to say. Just to HEAR the book of Revelation read
is a blessing ! Sure, much of it is difficult to understand, but so
constant are the glimpses of Christ in glory: so consistent the
outworking of the will of God: so glorious the ultimate
consummation, that just to hear the prophecies of this book
being read is a blessing in a troubled world like ours. But we
must also HEED what is written. To " keep," is to give " heed
to," " to watch over," " to observe attentively."

We must keep an eye on things in the light of what the
book has to say, for John says, " the time is at hand." (1:3)
Now this phrase is similar to the phrase in (1:1) where John
says, " The Revelation .... shortly come to pass." Of course
"shortly," does not mean " momentarily," because nearly two
millennia have passed since John wrote about these things.
Rather it means " suddenly," or " without warning." Now
that's what this phrase means, " the time is at hand," the things
prophesied in this book can happen at any time without
warning.

It is characteristic of John in his writings to put a key either
at the front or back door of the book, which will unlock its
meaning. In (1:19) we have:

(4) THE BIBLICAL OUTLINE OF THE BOOK

Now this verse contains the golden key to the book of
Revelation. It tells us that there is A PAST: A PRESENT: and A
FUTURE in this book. This is its threefold division and the
divisions are clear.

(a) " THE THINGS WHICH THOU HAST SEEN."

These words refer to the vision of the glorified Christ which
was just shown to John. This division constitutes chapter 1.

(b) " THE THINGS WHICH ARE."

These words refer to the letters to the seven churches and they compose chapters two and three, which have to do with this present era.

(c) " THE THINGS WHICH SHALL BE HEREAFTER."

Now to an unprejudiced mind it seems evident that the third section of the book commences here at (ch 4) And everything in the book from chapter four to the end, will occur after the church is taken out of the earth. These three divisions are clear and they do not overlap. Each division is complete in itself and distinct from the other two. This is God's own division of the book.

(5) THE CENTRAL FIGURE OF THE BOOK

THE CENTRAL PERSON of the book of Revelation is not John (as the title may lead you to believe) but Jesus Christ. This is a revelation of Jesus as told to John. And if we study the book of Revelation and don't learn anything about Christ, then we've misread the book of Revelation. Revelation is meant to be an unveiling of Christ to us, but it also tells of the time when Christ's glory will be unveiled, or revealed to all people. When Christ came to us the first time, His Glory was veiled but when He comes again, His glory will be completely unveiled. When studying the book of Revelation, it's very easy to become focused on trying to decipher and understand the prophecy. However, our main focus is to be on the One whose coming is prophesied. After all, it's not the Coming we want to be familiar with but the PERSON WHO IS COMING.

Imagine a train station. In that station there is a station master whose main objective is to know as much as possible about all the trains. And so he has all kinds of intricate charts to help him predict exactly where a train is and when it will reach the station. Imagine also that there is a young lady at the station. Now she is not nearly as well informed as the station master, but she knows that her fiancé is on the train that is about to arrive, and she can hardly wait for it to get there. Our hearts also need to beat in anticipation of the arrival of the King. You may find a justification for your point of view, or you may find reasons to support some fine point of prophecy, but if you don't see the Lord Jesus in the book of Revelation you've missed the real point. For this book is pre-eminently the revelation of Christ.

(a) HIS DIGNITY:

There is a reference to the TRINITY in (1:4-5 Isa 11:2) Christ is presented here:

(1) THE FAITHFUL WITNESS:

He came to earth to be a witness to a dark and degenerate world. It was He who said, " to this end was I born for this cause came I into the world that I should bear witness unto the truth." (John 18:37)

(2) THE FIRST BEGOTTEN OF THE DEAD:

" First begotten," (1:5) does not mean the first one raised from the dead but the highest of those raised from the dead. (Rom 8:29) Others had returned to life to die again. He ROSE and is ALIVE for evermore. (1:18) Is this not what a persecuted church needs to hear? (1:9) Is this not what those facing trials: difficulties, need to hear?

(3) THE PRINCE OF THE KINGS OF THE EARTH:

He is the King of Heaven: (Dan 4:37) the King of the Jews: (Matt 2:2) the King of Israel: (John 1:49) the King of the Ages: (1 Tim 1:17) the King of Glory: (Ps 24:7) the King of

Saints: (15:3) and the King of Kings (19:16) He is the mighty Prince of the Kings of the Earth. (Dan 8:25) The Lord is seen here in His three-fold OFFICE. PROPHET for He is the Faithful Witness. PRIEST for He is the first begotten of the dead, KING for He is the Prince of the kings of the earth. The Lord is seen in His three-fold WORK.

" Unto Him that loved us." (literally keeps on loving us) " and washed us." (literally once for all washed us) That's HIS PAST WORK OF REDEMPTION for He is the Faithful Witness.(1:6) " Kings and priests .... " That's HIS PRESENT WORK OF SANCTIFICATION for He is the First Begotten of the dead. " Behold He cometh with clouds." (1:7) That's HIS FUTURE WORK OF GLORIFICATION for He is the Prince of the kings of the earth.

(b) HIS DEITY:

" I am Alpha and Omega." (1:8) These are the first and last letters of the Greek alphabet. From A to Z, He is the beginning and the end and the one who encompasses the whole of creation. Nothing comes before Him. No one will come after Him. " For FROM Him and THROUGH Him and TO Him are all things." (Rom 11:36) " The Lord which is and which was and is to come." He is eternally the same PAST: PRESENT: and FUTURE. " The Almighty." Jesus Christ is God in every sense of the word. There is nothing He cannot do because there are no boundaries to His power.

(c) HIS DESCENT:

" Behold He cometh with clouds." (1:7) This describe's our Lords RETURN TO THE EARTH and must not be confused with His RETURN TO THE AIR to catch away his blood-bought people. (1 Thess 4:16) Here is an event that will be witnessed by the whole world and especially by a repentant nation of Israel. (Zech 12:10-12) He IS COMING present tense. (1:7) His Coming is NEAR.

A couple retired to bed for the evening. As they laid on their pillows, the grandfather clock downstairs began to chime. Ten o'clock ! Eleven o'clock ! Twelve o'clock ! but it continued to sound. Thirteen o'clock ! Fourteen o'clock ! Fifteen o'clock. Hearing all fifteen chimes, the husband popped his head up in amazement.

His wife asked him, "Honey, what time is it?"

"I don't know," he replied, "but its later than its ever been before."

None of us know the hour He is coming. But its later than its ever been before.

Chapter Two

The Coming Christ

❖

What the church needs today is a new awareness of Christ and His Glory. We need to see Him " high and lifted up." (Is 6:1) There is a dangerous absence of awe and worship in our church fellowships today. We are boasting about standing on our own feet, instead of breaking and falling at His feet. For years Evan Roberts the leader of the Welsh revival at the beginning of this century prayed, " Bend me, bend me," and when God answered, the great Welsh Revival resulted. The need of the hour is this, we must regain our vision of the sovereign authority of Jesus Christ. And this must begin in the church. We must see Him as HE IS .... enthroned: exalted: sovereign: ruling: reigning: and then we must be brought into humble submission to His LORDSHIP. Then and only then, will we experience that fresh movement of the Spirit of God that we so desperately need !

An aged man, probably in his nineties, John was the last living apostle. The year was about AD 95, and while imprisoned on Patmos John heard a loud voice like a trumpet speaking. The voice was none other than Jesus Christ ! John was told to record Christ's final call to His church. He was instructed to write in a book what he saw and heard and send it to seven churches in Asia Minor. But before John was told WHAT to write to the churches he was shown WHO is the HEAD of the church. The church must see Christ's sovereign Lordship before she hears what He says. As John turns to the voice he sees the awesome vision of Jesus Christ. Not the Lord Jesus as He once WAS: in the form of a lowly bond-servant, but Christ as He IS: the King of Kings and Lord of Lords. Here in (Rev 1) we see THE COMING CHRIST.

Now it may be that this vision of the Lord in (Rev 1) explains an interesting episode at the end of (John 21) when at the sea of Galilee the Risen Lord commissioned Peter with the words, " Feed my sheep," then prophesied that Peter would one day die a martyrs death. At that point Peter speaking of John said, " Lord and what shall this man do ?" (John 21:21) " Jesus saith unto him, if I will that he tarry till I come what is that to thee ? Follow me." Now because of a misunderstanding of this conversation between Peter and the Risen Lord, word went out among the disciples that John would never die, until the Lord returned. I wonder does (Rev 1) provide the explanation: John did remain alive to see the Coming of the Lord. He foresaw the Lord's Coming as an event in history, but He also saw it in the form of a vision from God.

Now tradition tells us that John lived to a ripe old age and was buried in Ephesus, but he did live to see the Coming of the Lord. He saw the Lord's Coming in symbols of royal garments: of brilliant light: of blazing fire: of thunderous sound: of supreme power, purity, wisdom and holiness. John saw THE COMING CHRIST.

(1) THE AWESOME SIGHT

The Book of Revelation is a book of symbols and these symbols are important.(1:3) In this opening chapter we discover truth conveyed in the form of symbols. The Lord Jesus is described in a way that is not intended to convey His actual physical appearance but various aspects of His character, His attributes and His role. It's interesting to notice the stages through which John passed in receiving this particular vision. In (1:10) he says " I heard," in (1:12) " I turned," in (1:12) " I saw," in (1:17) " I fell." Now the first thing that John does is to turn and see WHO is addressing him. (1:12-13)

What are the seven candlesticks ? " The mystery of the seven stars which thou sawest in my right hand, and the seven golden candlesticks. The seven stars are the angels of the seven churches: and the seven candlesticks which thou sawest are the seven churches."(1:20) And Christ walks in the Midst. The Lord Jesus was always in the midst. In the days of His childhood they found Him in the temple " sitting in the midst of the doctors." (Lk 2:46)

When they nailed Him to the Cross, Christ was " in the midst." (Matt 27:38) Today He says to us, " Where two or three are gathered together in My name there am I in the midst of them." (Matt 18:20) As the Lord of the Lampstands He walks in the midst of the churches. This is THE CENTRALITY OF CHRIST in relation to each local church.

What a revelation of Glory for an aged apostle who vividly remembered the garments that were stolen: the head that was crowned: the hands and feet that were pierced. How thrilling it must have been for John who had witnessed the SUFFERING OF CHRIST, now to see the GLORY OF CHRIST. They had tried to confine him physically on an island ten miles long and six miles wide but now he is transported away from it all and in the Spirit on the Lord's Day what better to begin with than with a sight of the Lord Himself. What compensation for an aged saint being denied the usual privileges of the Lord's Day. Who did John see ?

(a) THE RESURRECTED CHRIST:

" One like unto the Son of Man." (1:13) It was a full sixty years since John had at last seen Jesus. But he immediately recognised Him as " the Son of Man." (Dan 7:13-14) The Saviour has not changed. He became a man at His birth in Bethlehem, He was resurrected as a man, He ascended to heaven as a man, and He will return as a man. And so John recognised His Lord, THE RESURRECTED CHRIST, the Son of Man.

(b) THE REIGNING CHRIST:

The next thing that John noticed about the Lord Jesus was His clothing. He was clothed " with a garment down to the foot " (1:13) In ancient times, this was the recognised apparel of AUTHORITY: DIGNITY and RULERSHIP. In OT times, a long robe was the attire of spiritual leaders of high rank, whether it be the High Priest (Exod 25: Zech 3:4) a King (1 Sam 24:5) a Prince (Ezek 26:16) or a Judge. (Ezek 9:1) This was how John saw Christ. Wearing sovereign apparel. Bearing the garments of regal majesty. Adorned with absolute authority. His verdicts are undisputed. His authority is unlimited. His reign is unrivalled. From His clothing, John's focus looked upward to behold Christ's head and hair. He is:

(c) THE RIGHTEOUS CHRIST:

" His head and His hairs were white like wool, as white as snow." (1:14) This dazzling white is a symbol of Christ's absolute sinless holiness. (Dan 7:9) HOLINESS means SEPARATENESS ! It comes from a Semitic root that means " to cut." Something would be cut in half and the two parts separated. It means that Christ is SEPARATED from all mankind. He is a cut above us. Unlike us. Totally other than us. Infinitely perfect and pure. The Lord Jesus does not conform to any standard. HE IS THE STANDARD!

The Bible claims that Christ " knew no sin." (2 Cor 5:21) He " did no sin." (1 Pet 2:22) He " had no sin." (1 John 3:5) It is holiness that Christ requires of His church. We must be separated from the world .... different, not like the world. The Lord says, " Be ye holy for I am holy." (1 Pet 1:16) Despite the degenerating morals of our day Christ has not lowered His standard one iota. H. Bonar said, " I looked for the church and I found it in the world: I looked for the world and I found it in the church." While peering at Christ's head, John noticed His eyes. John saw Christ with fiery lasers flashing out of each socket. He is:

(d) THE REVEALING CHRIST:

" His eyes were as a flame of fire." (1:14) He has vision that penetrates .... or burns to the core. Today we might say He has X-ray vision. A.W. Tozer writes, " Because God knows all things perfectly, He knows no thing better than any other thing but all things equally well. He never discovers anything. He is never surprised, never amazed."

M. Henry wrote: " God not only sees men, He sees through them." He sees right through us. He knows about everything we've done. He knows about every thought we've ever had. He hears every lie we utter. Unlike any earthly Judge the Lord Jesus cannot be deceived. There was a story of a country man who was arrested for stealing a watch. At his trial, the prosecution did everything they could to prove the mans guilt but there was not enough evidence. He could not be found guilty so the judge told him, " Sam you've been acquitted. You can go home." The man replied, " Does that mean I have to give the watch back ?"

The Lord Jesus cannot be deceived. Nothing escapes His attention. He never has to gather information or ask questions. He never learns anything. Who would teach Him ? He sees every MINISTER: notes every MEMBER observes every MINISTRY: views every MOTIVE with X-ray vision. From His fiery eyes John looks down to His red-hot feet, feet that are glowing like burnished metal in a fiery furnace. He is:

(e) THE RELENTLESS CHRIST:

" And His feet like unto fine brass." (1:15) Brass in the Bible symbolises judgment. When Moses lifted up a brass serpent in the wilderness, it was a foreshadowing of the cross where the Lord Jesus would become sin under judgment for us. (John 3:14) Here Christ's feet, which appear as burnished brass, are going forth to judge. He is unstoppable: there will be no escape from the wrath of God when Jesus' burning feet touch the earth. But even today He will judge sin wherever He finds it. ESPECIALLY in the church. (2:4 14-15 20 3:1 15-16)   Christ ESPECIALLY hates sin in His own spiritual family. More so than in the world. Make no mistake THE HEAD OF THE CHURCH will judge sin in His churches. " For the time is come that judgment must begin at the house of God."(1 Pet 4:17)

Now up to this point John has tried to describe the APPEARANCE of the Lord Jesus but now he moves from SIGHT TO SOUND and he sees:

(f) THE REGAL CHRIST:

For he says that the sound of Jesus' voice is " as the sound of many waters." (1:15) He speaks with a voice like mighty ocean waves crashing against the jagged rocks of Patmos! David says that " The voice of the Lord is upon the waters: The God of glory thundereth: the Lord is upon many waters. The voice of the Lord is powerful: the voice of the Lord is full of majesty." (Ps 29:3-4) Imagine arguing with Niagara Falls. Imagine standing at the foot of the Falls with some twelve million cubic feet of water roaring down each minute and trying to argue with a thunderous voice like that. One day soon that voice as the sound of many waters, will break the silence with a roar, and all voices raised in angry protest will be silenced, drowned out by His. This is THE CHRIST WHO IS COMING. He is not coming as the bloodied and beaten Saviour but as the King of Kings and Lord of Lords.

(g) THE REGULATING CHRIST:

" And He had in his right hand seven stars." (1:16) Who or what are these stars ? " The seven stars are the angels of the seven churches." Angel (angelos) means," a divinely commissioned messenger." One sent from God with a message. The Lord Jesus is holding the seven stars in His right hand, the hand of power and that suggests that He has complete control of all things. He is the regulator of the universe. God is still in control: God's still running the show: God is still on the throne! One day Christ will restore permanent order and harmony to His creation ! The vision unfolds further and John notes that out of His mouth proceeds a deadly weapon .... a sword. For He is:

(h) THE REVENGING CHRIST:

" And out of His mouth went a sharp two-edged sword." (1:16)

The sword is the, Word of God. (Eph 6:17 Heb 4:12) Nothing can stand before God's Word. Ten times in (Gen 1) we read, " And God said." Flaming suns sprang into being, and life in many forms arose vibrant from the dust. When the " Word was made flesh," (John 1:14) demons, disease, and death fled. Whether it is the Word going forth to REPLENISH THE EARTH as in (Gen 1) or to REDEEM THE EARTH as in the days of His flesh, or to RECLAIM THE EARTH as here in this majestic scene, the result is always the same. Whether as CREATOR: COMFORTER: or CONQUEROR that Mighty Word is invincible. Finally, John sees Christ's face shining with the glory of God. He is:

(i) THE RESPLENDENT CHRIST:

" And His countenance was as the sun shineth in his strength." (1:16) Once that face was marred and spat upon, here it shines in resplendent glory.(Matt 17:2) It is this Divine

Glory that John now beholds. Unveiled. Unmasked. Unadulterated. (John 17:5) What a vision of Christ. This is THE COMING CHRIST.

(2) THE ABJECT SERVANT

The effect of this dazzling sight upon John was nothing less than paralyzing. Before such an awesome sight, what could John do, what could any human being do, but fall at the feet of Christ as though dead. John had once walked with Christ for three years. He had witnessed His miracles and heard His sermons. He had leaned upon His breast in the Upper Room and watched Him die on the Cross. Finally he had rejoiced in His resurrection and viewed His ascension. But that had all happened some 60 years before. Now as he sees the Resplendent Redeemer in all His blinding brightness he drops at His feet as a dead man.

(a) HIS HUMBLE SUBMISSION

" And when I saw him I fell at His feet." (1:17) Immediately, John collapsed to the ground, left to grovel on the floor. Every nerve fibre in his body was trembling. He was looking for a place to hide. ANYWHERE to get out from under the holy gaze of Christ. But there was no place to hide. John lay exposed before Christ. UNDONE. UNMASKED. UNRAVELED. The holiness of Christ exposed John's own unholiness. He caught one glimpse of the Holy One and his self-esteem was shattered! Was it not the same for Isaiah? When he saw the SOVEREIGNTY: PURITY: AUTHORITY of the LORD JESUS he cried, " Woe is me for I am undone." (Isa 6:5 John 12:41)

Was it not the same for Peter? After a long days fishing endeavour, the Saviour told Simon to shove back out and let down his nets again. Simon snapped back, " Lord you stick to the preaching and let us do the fishing." Begrudgingly, Peter launched out. But to his amazement, his catch was so big that their nets began to break. When Peter saw this he realised he was standing in the presence of a Holy God. Instantly he fell at Jesus' feet, " Depart from me for I am a sinful man, O Lord." (Lk 5:9)

A vision of the glorified Christ will always drive us to our knees. Like John we must find ourselves at His feet. Lower and lower we must descend, driven downward by His Divine Presence. When we compare ourselves with others, we seem RESPECTABLE. But when we see ourselves in comparison to Him, we are RUINED. Shaken down to our roots. The closer we draw to the Light, the more the dirt of our own heart is exposed. This must be the posture of the church .... flat on our faces before the Lord.

(b) HIS HOLY FEAR:

" And when I saw him I fell at his feet AS DEAD." (1:17) John collapsed at Jesus' feet as A DEAD MAN. He was speechless: motionless: and all shook up. Solomon wrote, " the fear of the Lord is the beginning of knowledge." (Prov 1:7) A FEAR OF GOD. Let's face it. There's too little fear of God in our churches today. But a true vision of Christ will instil us with HOLY FEAR.

Some years ago Queen Elizabeth was visiting in Los Angeles. She was being taken through some of the most underprivileged neighbourhoods. As she approached one project area in a ghetto she asked her driver to stop. When he did she got out of the car unannounced and went into a very poor apartment chosen at random. The lady of the house was overwhelmed. The Queen in her humble abode. Unaware of the proper protocol appropriate for addressing royalty, she did not know to curtsy or bow, nor did she know to address the Queen as Her Majesty. Instead when she approached the

Queen she wrapped both arms around her giving the Queen a warm bear hug. The Queen's entourage was appalled. The media was shocked. The Secret Service was aghast. No one touches the Queen. This woman had no idea how to address Royalty. There was no fear. No awe. No respect. Consequently her approach was inappropriate. Is that not where we are in the church today ? No fear. No awe. No reverence. May HOLY FEAR fill the church again.

(3) THE ABSOLUTE SOVEREIGN

As John lay prostrate before the feet of Christ, the Lord did something that was typical of Him: He reached down and touched John.

(a) HE CONVEYS HIS SYMPATHY:

" And He laid his right hand upon me, saying unto me, fear not." (1:17) As you read through the Gospels you see that Christ was always touching people. When He healed a leper He touched him. When He restored sight to the blind, He put His hands upon their eyes. The touch of His Hand brought His strengthening grace. No wonder Christ reaches out and touches John. The elderly apostle, now in his nineties, has almost died of a heart attack because the Lord unveiled His Glory. He needs to be RESTORED AND REASSURED. Now in order to comfort John, Christ gives a fuller revelation of Himself. You see true strength always comes from a deeper knowledge of Christ and so:

(b) HE REVEALS HIS IDENTITY:

Here are staggering claims for Deity, uttered by our Lord. The idea is, " John look to me and be comforted."

(1) " I AM "

John would recall those words " I AM." John himself recorded the series of " I AM," claims in his gospel. " I am the bread of life," (John 6:35) and so on. " I AM," was the divine name that God chose for Himself. " And God said unto Moses, I AM THAT I AM: and He said, thus shalt thou say unto the children of Israel, I AM hath sent me unto you." (Exod 3:14) Not " I was that I was," nor " I will be that I will be." But, " I AM THAT I AM," the self-existent eternal, sovereign God. In taking this name the Lord Jesus is claiming, in no uncertain terms to be GOD!

(2) " THE FIRST AND THE LAST "

In the OT God said, " I am the first, and I am the last and beside me there is no God." (Isa 44:6 48:12) By saying, " I am the first," Christ lays claim to eternal preexistence. By saying, " I am the last," He is eternally immutable. He is the same " yesterday, and today, and forever." (Heb 13:8)

(3) " THE LIVING ONE "

" I am he that liveth." or " I am the Living One." (1:18) That was another name that was applied to God. To Joshua God said, " Hereby ye shall know that the Living God is among you." (Jos 3:10) Peter used this name to describe God, " Thou art the Christ the Son of the LIVING GOD." (Matt 16:16) Clearly when the Lord Jesus takes this title He is saying, " I am God." " John there's nothing to fear. I have conquered sin, death, Satan, and hell. I am alive forever."

(c) HE AFFIRMS HIS AUTHORITY:

" And have the keys of hell and of death." (1:18) Christ's keys signify His sovereign authority to open and close the grave. He decides WHO DIES WHEN! And He alone can get them out. " John I have all power over death. You're not finished yet. Your life is not yet over. I'm not yet ready to take the key and put it into the door of death for you." Christ will be with us to the end: in the end: and beyond the end. This is the CHRIST WHO IS COMING What a Saviour!

Chapter Three

The Church that Left its Love

❖

The Austrian composer Franz Joseph Haydn was a man with a cheerful disposition despite the fact that he was married to a bitter and malicious woman. She continually belittled both Haydn and his music. Several times, purely out of spite, she stole the only existing copies of his music from his desk and destroyed them. Haydn spent much of his career travelling around Europe .... partly because his talents were in such a demand throughout the Continent, but also because travel gave him time away from his disagreeable wife. During a visit to England on one occasion, a friend visited Haydn in his rented room in London.

This friend noticed a large stack of unopened letters on Haydn's desk and asked the composer why he did not open his mail. " All of those letters are from my wife,"

Haydn jovially explained. " We write to each other every week but I do not open her letters, and I am sure she does not open mine."

In Revelation chapters 2 and 3 we find a stack of letters, seven in all, which have largely lain ignored and unopened by the Christian church over the years. Many people tend to skip over these seven letters to the churches, so eager are they to hurry on to those juicy, action-packed blood-and-thunder sections of Revelation. We would rather hear about the great cataclysms of the last days than be confronted with the urgent challenge of our own present moment. How tragic! These seven letters to seven churches are powerful letters, burning with urgency. Their message is still as vital and timely today as when first written. Now we can view these churches before us in a three-fold manner.

(1) WE CAN VIEW THEM HISTORICALLY:

First and foremost these are seven letters written to seven actual, historical churches found in the Roman province of Asia, which was located on the Western seaboard of what we now know as Turkey. Geographically these seven cities form a rough circle and they are listed here in the order which a messenger might visit them. Sailing from Patmos he would arrive at Ephesus, then he would travel north to Smyrna and Pergamum and then south east to Thyatira: Sardis: Philadelphia and Laodicea. So the Risen Lord had a direct message to seven literal churches existing at that time.

(2) WE CAN VIEW PROPHETICALLY:

The plan of the book seems to indicate this. (1:19) " The things which thou hast seen" chapter 1. " The things which are." - chapters 2-3 " The things which shall be hereafter." chapters 4-22. So chapters 2 and 3 reveal to us conditions in the church from Pentecost to the Rapture. In other words each church may be seen as representing a different phase in church history. (1:3)

(3) WE CAN VIEW THEM TYPICALLY:

One might ask the question, why are only SEVEN churches addressed ? Why THESE particular seven ? Certainly there were more than seven churches in the area ? (Col 1:2 4:13 Acts 20:5) Other churches could have been chosen. But the Lord chose these seven churches because they represent conditions that have prevailed throughout church history, from the beginning to the end. Any condition of any church in any place at any time may be found here.

Now the first of these seven letters is addressed to Ephesus if for no better reason than because it was nearer to Patmos than the other six cities, yet Ephesus was more than the nearest city, it had a distinction all of its own. Its citizens liked to call it " THE METROPOLIS OF ASIA." This was a very prosperous business centre because it was situated on the trade route from Rome to the East. Four major roadways intersected at Ephesus, bringing businessmen and merchants from the important cities of the Roman provinces.

Ephesus was also a centre of Pagan Worship. One of the seven wonders of the ancient world was located here in Ephesus .... the Temple of Diana, a massive structure that was as long as two football fields. With Temple worship there not only came IDOLATRY but IMMORALITY. Small wonder businessmen travelled the four major roadways to Ephesus. They came flocking into the Temple to have their every sexual fantasy fulfilled.

Ephesus became known as " THE VANITY FAIR OF THE ANCIENT WORLD." Yet it was there, in the midst of that godless city, that God planted a church. Paul recognised the stratgeic importance of this city and went there on his third missionary journey. (Acts 19-20) He spent three years establishing the work of God. Timothy also laboured there building on the spiritual foundation laid by his spiritual father (1 Tim 1:3) and " according to an early tradition the apostle John replaced Timothy toward the end of the first century as leader of this church." This church had enjoyed the labours ,of the best and most gifted men, but then gifted and godly ministers are no guarantee of a church's spiritual progress. Indeed while this church had enjoyed some "STELLAR MINISTRY," the Lord reminded them that He was in control of the ministry placing the " stars," where He pleased.

How easy it is for a church to become proud and forget that pastors/teachers are God's gifts who may be taken away at any time. (Eph 4:11) Now Ephesus was a very privileged church, the only church in the NT to which two apostles addressed letters. " When Paul wrote to Ephesus it was THE CLIMAX CHURCH of the day .... when John wrote some 20-30 years later it was THE CRISIS CHURCH of the day." " I have somewhat against thee, because thou hast left thy first love." (2:4) They had not LOST their FUNDAMENTAL-ISM but they had LAPSED into FORMALISM, they had not quit THEIR FERVENT LABOURING, but they had left their FIRST LOVE. The honeymoon was over.

(1) THEIR VITAL MINISTRY: COMMENDATION

How gracious of the Risen Lord to start with words of COMMENDATION. (2:1) The word " angel," means messenger. J. Vernon McGee writes: " It could refer to a member of the angelic host of heaven: it could refer to a ruler or teacher of the congregation. Personally, I think that it refers to the local pastors. It is good to hear a pastor being called an angel .... sometimes we are called other things." Now notice the description of the Lord here.

HIS PROTECTION: " He holdeth." (2:1) In (ch 1) He HAS the stars, in (ch 2) he HOLDS the stars. The word " hold," indicates keeping all of something in one's hand, like grasping a small coin within one's fist. We are protected, surrounded and encompassed by Christ's care.

HIS PRESENCE: " He walketh." (2:1) He walks with and among His churches. How challenging. Every detail of every church is known to Him.

HIS PLACE: " in the midst." (2:1) His PLACE must be CENTAL and PREEMINENT.

HIS PERCEPTION: " I know." (2:2) because He knows he proceeds to give each church an " X ray," of its condition. What did he know about Ephesus ? What did He commend them for ?

(a) SELFLESS AND SACRIFICIAL:

Christianity was no spectator sport here. They didn't come to church to be entertained. They were actively involved in the work of ministry. Sacrifically. Selflessly. Serving. Doing. Toiling. Giving. Going. The word " works," in (2:2) means " activities," " labour," " toil," " patience," " endurance " or " perseverance." In other words they served Christ to the point of exhaustion. Holy sweat rolled down their foreheads as they ministered in His name. " Perseverance," (hupomone) means they ministered under much stress and pressure. When they took on a task, they stuck with it until the job was finished.

Teaching the Bible. Reaching souls. Supporting one another. Feeding the poor. Doing the ministry right and left. No lazy loafers at Ephesus. This is very Christlike. For the Lord Jesus came not to be served, but to serve (Mk 10:45) Good deeds: selfless toil: long days: draining hours, exerting Himself to the point of exhaustion.

(b) STRICT AND SOUND:

" And how thou canst not bear them which are evil." (2:2) They set a high moral standard and chose not to tolerate sin in the camp. If one of their member slipped into sin, they would approach that person, lovingly confront him, and call him to repentance. If that person wouldn't repent, the church would not allow this leaven to spread to the whole lump. This was no spiritual country club. They didn't look like saints on Sunday and act like aints on Monday. They were serious about their walk with Christ. Do you know why we are so weak and feeble in these days ? Discipline has gone. (Acts 5:1 1 Cor 5:1)

The Lord went on, " And thou hast tried them which say they are apostles, and are not, and hast found them liars." Paul warned this church. " For I know this, that after my departing shall grievous wolves enter in among you, not sparing the flock." (Acts 20:29) What happened was this. When travelling preachers came to Ephesus, their doctrine was put to the test before they could get into the pulpit. Doctrinal error would not be tolerated here. They called a spade a spade. They could smell a heretic a mile off. When they heard theological error, alarms went off. Flares went up. False teachers were give an apple and a road map.

Nicolaitan (2:6) means " to conquer the people," and some people think John was speaking here about the growing distinction between clergy and laity, a false distinction that is nowhere taught in the NT (1 Pet 2:9 Rev 1:6) What a church this was. This was a citadel of orthodoxy. A bastion of truth. A fortress for the faith. Is this important ? Absolutely. The church that stands for nothing will fall for anything. Any ministry can only be as strong as its doctrinal purity. Like the foundation of a house, theological correctness provides stability, strength, and longevity. Some will say we are judgmental but Scripture says, " Test the spirits," " Prove all things, hold fast that which is good." (1 John 4:1 1 Thes 5:21)

(c) STEADFAST AND STRONG:

" And hast borne, and hast patience, and for my name's sake hast laboured and hast not fainted." (2: 3) Despite growing opposition to Christ, this church remained rock-solid. They wouldn't waver from their mission. While living in the hub of paganism, they held tenaciously to their witness for Christ. Even their motives were right. They endured for Christ's name sake, not their own. They served for His glory, not their own reputation. Toiling. Persevering. Strict. Sound. Steadfast.

Strong. This place was hopping. What could possibly be wrong with a church like this ? Plenty. They had everything but the main thing. Love.

(2) THEIR PERSONAL DEFICIENCY: ACCUSATION:

How abruptly, the Lord changes the tone of this letter. The Master puts his finger on the one glaring deficiency in this church that threatened to ruin everything else. " Nevertheless I have somewhat against thee, because thou hast left thy first love." (2:4) Now the word, " thou," must be counted singular and plural. The whole church had left their first love but they did it one by one.

(a) THIS WAS CRITICAL:

It always hurts when someone has something against you. But when Christ does, that's serious. Something was missing. This church had left its first love. Amid the Ephesians many ministries, and their tenacious stand for the truth, their love for Christ had grown cold. The more busy they became, the further they drifted away from simple devotion to Christ.

This was labour without love, doctrine without devotion, teaching without tenderness, activity without affection. It was so serious that it endangered the church's very existence. (2:5)

(b) THIS WAS GRADUAL:

Thirty years before John wrote these seven letters, Paul wrote the Ephesian epistle and in that letter there are at least twenty references to love. When Paul wrote to them he reminded them of their exalted position, " Ye are RISEN." (Eph 2:6) Now the Risen Lord says, " Thou art FALLEN." (2:5) The word " left," pictures something GRADUAL ! This departure didn't happen overnight. Somewhere along the way they lost their passion.

Interestingly enough this church was located in a city which was the chief port of Asia Minor. Its harbor was given to much change because of its continual silting .... what was water became land, what was land became water. And the shifting character of the city was reflected in the church. Once they were in love with Christ, but now they have fallen out of love.

A Christian was driving home from church. The wife was sitting in the front seat on the far left side. Her husband was in his usual place behind the steering wheel. Seemingly a large gulf separated them. With lonely eyes she looked at him and said, " Dear, do you remember when we first met, how close we used to sit to each other ? You used to put you arm around me. What happened to those days?" With one hand firmly attached to the steering wheel and the other resting on the empty space between them, he said, " Well, I haven't moved." The distance was not because he had moved. A separation resulted because she had moved away. She had left her first love ! That's precisely what happened in the Ephesian church. Over the years they had left their first love!

It's so easy for ministry to become mechanical, relationship to become routine, doxology to slip back into cold orthodoxy. A person can have lots of activity FOR Christ, but little intimacy WITH Christ.

(c) THIS WAS FUNDAMENTAL:

What does our Lord mean when He says " Thou hast left thy first love." (2:4) What is our first love ? It's the love we felt for the Saviour when we first came to know Him. Fervent. Personal. Excited. Uninhibited. Adventuresome. Reckless. Its that wonderful sense of discovery that He loves us, that He has delivered us, that He has freed us from our sins. Once our hearts went out to Him in gratitude. Once we had eyes for no one but the Saviour. Ever watch a young couple in love? See how they talk to each other, how they touch each other's hands, how their eyes meet. Talk to them and they probably won't even hear you. They are "spaced out." They are lost in each other. They are thinking only of the wonder of each other.

Thats the way it seemed to be when the world's most eligible bachelor, Prince Charles, Duke of Windsor exchanged wedding vows with the beautiful Lady Diana Spencer. It was all something of a fairy tale. A starry eyed script that could have been written in Hollywood. With 750 million viewers watching around the globe via satellite, with the streets of London lined with thousands of admirers all craning their necks to get a glimpse of the newly wedded royal couple. Off they dashed to their honeymoon. Full of life. Full of love. Full of hope. But that was THEN.

For the clock struck twelve on this real-life Cinderella story. Somewhere along the way their lives grew apart. Their love grew cold. Stale. Stagnant. Mechanical. Routine. The fact is, the honeymoon is over. The glow is gone. The Royal romance is a thing of the past. This can happen us spiritually. Once our hearts were so full of passion and excitement. Bible study was so life-changing. Prayer was so heart-lifting. Worship was so real. But that was THEN. What about NOW?

(3) THEIR SPIRITUAL RECOVERY: RESTORATION

With arms wide open, Christ prescribes the steps that lead back to the honeymoon stage. Practically speaking, here is how we again draw close to Him. Here is how to rekindle our lost passion for Christ. Here's how to fall back in love with the Saviour.

(a) REMEMBER:

" Remember from whence thou art fallen." (2:5) Literally, " keep on remembering." To look back can be sinful (Lot's wife) but it can also be sensible. Remember back to when you first came to Christ. Replay that initial excitement. Refocus on those times when you really loved the Saviour. Remember the freshness of your first love. Remember when it was spring-time in your soul. Remember how you yearned to learn more of the Word. Remember when your heart was filled with love for Christ. Remember when you loved your fellow-believers. Remember when you had a passion for souls. The road back to Christ begins by first Remembering. Memory is the handmaid of revival.

(b) REPENT:

" And repent." (2:5) After you remember, repent. That means to change the direction of your life. It is a change of heart. A change of mind. A change of will. It means to head back to the way things once were. It is a turning round and coming back to Christ. The fact is this, someone or something has replaced your first love. It's not that you don't have a first love anymore. It's that you have a new first love. It's no longer Christ. Anything that we love more than we love Christ is our new first love.

(c) REPEAT:

" Do the first works." (2:5) In other words, " Get back to the basics." What are these first works ? The Risen Lord does not specifically tell us here, but we can discover what they are from other New Testament Scriptures. Concerning the early believers we read, " They continued steadfastly in the apos-tles doctrine, and fellowship, and in breaking of bread, and in prayers. (Acts 2:42) It is these spiritual disciplines that lead us back to full love for Christ.

The Risen Lord says, if we do not Remember, Repent, and Repeat, there will be Removal. " I will come unto thee quickly and will remove thy candlestick out of his place." (2: 5) This is not the Second Coming, but the Lords coming in judgment to this church. If there is no Love, there will no Light. The reason for the church's existence has vanished, and Christ will say, " Turn out the lights, the party's over." History records the sad fact that Christ did indeed later remove the lampstand of the church in Ephesus. It has been gone for centuries, smothered by the Moslems. Today there is no local church within miles of Ephesus.

What is the home where love has died? What's the church where love has died? It's just a beautiful building with expensive furnishings. Are there not many places like that today? But the Lampstand has been removed for no ray of light ever radiates from that place. It has no Light because it has no Love. Without first love we can have Activity, Orthodoxy, and purity but there'll be no light shining from our churches. REMOVAL instead of REVIVAL.

If the entire church would not respond the hope is that individuals would. When Adam fell he lost access to the Tree of Life. Here's a fallen church. It has lost the paradise of bliss which comes from walking with God.

Chapter Four

A Church Under Pressure

❖

A line has been drawn in the sand. Sides have been taken, and war has been declared. Hell is officially in session. And the church is under attack. With mounting hostility, the kingdom of Satan is engaging in a full scale war against the church of Jesus Christ. The foul forces of darkness are escalating their campaign against the people of God with an unholy vengeance. Like two weather fronts colliding, a violent storm is brewing across the horizon as never before. Witness for example the scene at Hamilton Square Baptist Church in San Francisco. As church members gathered for their evening service on September 19th 1993, they knew it would be an eventful service. They just didn't know how eventful. The guest preacher for the evening was Lou Sheldon, an outspoken opponent of pro-homosexual legislation in California. As chairman of the Traditional Values Coalition, Sheldon had played a key role in overturning a 1989 partners ordinance in San Francisco.

As he came to speak, this church turned into a battleground. Two pro-homosexual newspapers had publicised Sheldons visit, leading to a barrage of phone calls to the church offices all week. Militant homo-sexual activists promised to show up in force and threatened to disrupt the service. And disrupt they did. The service became a war zone. Like an invading army, approximately 100 rioters stormed the church ground and took complete control of the exterior property. Angry protestors denied worshippers entrance into the church. Physical contact was used. One church member, a woman, was physically and forcibly carried away from the church's entrance by the activists.

All the while, the police stood by watching. Rioters vandalised church property. The church's Christian flag, was replaced by a homosexual flag. Innocent children were verbally harassed and threatened. Vile obscenities were yelled. When the service began angry gays pounded on the doors outside the sanctuary, taunting worshippers to come outside and join them in their sexual orgies. As the believers sang, the demonstrators threw eggs and rocks at the stained-glass windows. The pastor was pelted by debris and needed a police escort as he left in a church van. Sounds a bit like Sodom and Gomorrah. But this is America. Today. The most powerful nation in the Western world. What's next ?

Will this militant aggression by homosexual activists against the church continue ? What other " minorities," will join their cause and level their assault upon the church ? One thing is absolutely clear. The Lord Jesus warned us it would be this way. Before His own crucifixion, the Saviour told us, "If the world hate you, ye know that it hated me before it hated you. If ye were of the world, the world would love his own: but because ye are not of the world, but I have chosen you out of the world, therefore the world hateth you." (John 15:19) No mistaking it .... the world will hate us. Paul echoed the same truth, " This know also, that in the last days perilous times shall come .... yea and all that will live godly in Christ

Jesus shall suffer persecution." (2 Tim 3:12) A line has been drawn in the sand. Sides have been taken. And war has been declared. Hell is in direct conflict with Heaven.

Now the church at Smyrna knew all about this. Our Lord's second letter is addressed to the church at Smyrna .... A CHURCH UNDER PRESSURE. Smyrna represents every persecuted church in every age, and every persecuted believer in every cultural setting. Let's take a trip back to ancient Smyrna.

(1) THE SETTING OF THIS CHURCH

Today Smyrna is the third largest city in Turkey and a major international trade centre, as well as the home of the Nato southern command headquarters and the prestigious Aegean University. The city is now known as Izmir, but during the first century when the Book of Revelation was written, its name was Smyrna. Smyrna was situated 35 miles up the coast from Ephesus and it was the next city the postman would reach on his circular tour of the seven churches.

(a) ARCHITECTURALLY Smyrna was FAMOUS:

Prince Charles would have approved of the layout of this city. This was easily the most beautiful city in all of Asia Minor, " the crown of Asia." It was fronted by the coast of the Aegean Sea and flanked by a circular hill called the Pagos. This beautiful hill elevated above the city was outlined with a street called " The Street of Gold." On this street were pagan temples and stately public buildings which gave the appearance of a jewelled crown. The streets were well-paved and lined with groves of trees, enhancing its majesty beauty.

Because of their symmetrical arrangement, these buildings were called " the crown of Smyrna," because from afar off they looked like a necklace of jewels. Years earlier, Alexander the Great had determined to make Smyrna the model Greek city. To many it was. With such a noble beginning, Smyrna had blossomed into a city of advanced culture. A place where the arts: education: philosophy, and the sciences flourished. Proudly, " First in Asia in beauty and size," was inscribed on their coins. Few would argue.

(b) ECONOMICALLY Smyrna was FLOURISHING:

It had a natural landlocked harbour where entire fleets could be sheltered from outside attack. This great harbour allowed it to be second only to Ephesus in exports. As a result, Smyrna was a large, flourishing centre of international commerce and trade with a prosperous economy.

(c) POLITICALLY Smyrna was FAITHFUL:

This was a city that was renowned for its faithfulness to Rome. When six cities competed for the privilege to erect a temple to Rome, Smyrna was chosen over the others. Her allegiance to Caesar was unquestioned. Now because of all this, Smyrna was a thriving centre for Roman emperor worship. In that day, Caesar was a god to the people. His image was carved in marble and set before the city along with burning incense. Every citizen was called upon to publicly worship and confess allegiance to Rome's ruler annually. Anyone who refused would be severely punished, immediately imprisoned, and executed by the sword. What were the believers to do? They were faced with a choice. CAESAR or CHRIST ? To confess CAESAR meant LIBERTY, to confess CHRIST as Lord meant possible death !

In addition to all of this Smyrna was a hotbed of pagan worship. Temples to Cybele, Apollo, Asclepias, Aphrodite, and Zeus were built there. Greek gods and goddesses were openly worshipped. What a contrast there must have been between the humble meeting houses of the believers and the glory of the temples of the gods of Greece. Smyrna was no easy place

(b) THEY WERE ATTACKED ECONOMICALLY:

" I know thy POVERTY." (2:9) In Greek there are two words for poverty. The first (penia) describes the man who has nothing to spare, nothing extra. The second (ptocheian) describes the man who has nothing at all. That's the word that is used here. That's how poor this little church was. So poor they couldn't begin to make ends meet. Financially destitute, they didn't have a penny to their name. The reason? Well, todays health and wealth movement would answer, " because they were outside the will of God, all they had to do was name it and claim it." They were living beneath their privileges. God wanted them wealthy. Perhaps they should have been rebuked for their poverty? No. They suffered poverty because they were in the will of God! Financial prosperity is not God's will for everyone. Sometimes it costs to be a Christian.

Economically Smyrna was flourishing. No recession in the economy there. Everyone else in Smyrna was prospering. Yet, these Christian business men were being sacked from their jobs. Their premises were being broken into. Their goods stolen. Why ? They confessed Jesus Christ to be LORD. Not Caesar. Here they were Destitute. But Christ said " but thou art RICH." (2:9) The church at Smyrna was MATERIALLY POOR but SPIRITUALLY RICH . Laodicea was MATERIALLY RICH but SPIRITUALLY POOR. Which would you rather be? Like Smyrna or Laodicea ? Incidentally Christ's set of values is different from the worlds. " POOR BUT RICH."

We can lack much of this world's goods yet be "rich toward God," "rich in faith," "rich in good works," "have treasure in heaven." (Lk 12:21 James 2:25   1 Tim 6:18   Matt 6:19)

(c) THEY WERE ATTACKED RELIGIOUSLY:

Our Lord says, "I know the blasphemy of them which say they are Jews, and are not, but are the synagogue of Satan." (2:9) In Smyrna, there was a large Jewish community that was fanatically hostile against Christianity. They were even blaspheming the believers. " Blasphemy," means slander or speaking against. You see what happened was this. The Jews were beginning to spread lies about the believers, whose reputations were being ruined. They were slandering the Christians, planting lies, stirring up opposition. As at the crucifixion of Christ, these Jewish leaders were inciting the crowd against the Christians. Because these believers celebrated the Lord's Supper, the Jews accused them of eating human flesh.

Because this church refused to worship the gods who were enshrined in the pagan temples, they were called atheists. Christians talked about being members of one another, of loving one another, so they were accused of engaging in sexual orgies. They also accused the Christians of breaking up families because their message called for a highest allegiance to Christ. These Jews, said the Lord were the " synagogue of Satan." They were instruments of the Devil, used by hell to oppose the people and programmes of God.

History informs us that the church has often been perse-cuted by bigoted religionists. Think of the zeal of the Romanists against the Reformers. Think of the apostate churches in our land that are no more than synagogues of Satan. Satan goes to church just like Christians. Every Sunday the devil says, " I've got some of my preachers I want to hear speak. I've got some of my choirs I want to hear sing. I've got some disciples with whom I want to fellowship this morning." These churches are the strong-holds of Satan. They do not preach the true Gospel of Christ. They deny the inerrancy of Scripture. They cast scorn on the resurrection of Jesus Christ. They have forsaken the Word of God. They are contemplating ordaining homo-sexuals into the ministry. These " churches," are hellholes, instruments of the devil himself.

(d) THEY WERE ATTACKED PHYSICALLY:

" Fear none .... ten days." (2:10) This church had suffered. This church would suffer. In fact, the Lord guaranteed that the devil was about to cast some of them into prison. Roman prisons were ghastly places. Those imprisoned did not stay long. Either the prison authorities put you to death, or you were severely tortured and flung back onto the streets. Either way nobody stayed long in a Roman prison. The church in Smyrna PHYSICALLY SUFFERED. The Roman officials broke into their homes and arrested the believers before the startled eyes of their family. They dragged them off into Roman prisons and made public examples out of them before a watching world.

Christ said they would have, " tribulation ten days." Some Bible students have speculated that these ten days are symbolic of ten successive eras of Roman emperors, or ten consecutive stages of church history. Whatever the precise meaning of " the ten days, " we can be encouraged to know that " THE LORD SETS THE LIMITS TO OUR SUFFERING." The Lord is Sovereign in every situation. If the Lord says the test will last ten days then there is no force on earth that could make it last eleven days. You see no suffering can engulf us except with His Permission. God would say to the devil in Smyrna, "Thus far and no further." The devil is under the CONTROL and SOVEREIGNTY of Him who walks in the midst of the candlesticks and the gates of hell shall never against His church prevail ! Behind all persecution, whether Political, Economic, Religious stands Satan himself.

(e) THEY WERE ATTACKED SATANICALLY:

He's referred to as Satan in (2:9) and the Devil in (2:10) They were at war with hell itself. (Eph 6:11-12) Behind the Roman Empire stood the Evil Empire. The Devil unleashed his hellish hated against believers by inciting unbelievers to be filled with extreme hatred toward them. The result ? Imprisonment, for many death. This church suffered deeply. Simultaneously, they SUFFERED PERSECUTION on, not one, or two but five fronts. They were attacked Politically: Economically: Religiously: Physically: and Satanically. It is interesting to observe that there is no REBUKE for this church. Out of the seven churches, the Risen Lord rebukes five of them. But for two churches there is no criticism. The other church is Philadelphia. That was another Persecuted church. The lesson is clear. Persecution Purifies the Church.

The greatest blessing that could ever happen to the cause of Christ might be for the church to be persecuted ! Someone has said;

" The problem with Christians these days is no one wants to kill them anymore." Such persecution would melt us down to the bare essentials of what it means to be a genuine follower of the Lord Jesus. How was this church in Smyrna going to make it ? How were they going to bear up in the trials ahead ?

(3) THE SUSTAINING OF THIS CHURCH

Christ says, " Fear none of those things which thou shalt suffer." (2: 10) In the place of their FEARFULNESS the Lord wanted their FAITHFULNESS. The psalmist said, " What time I am afraid I will trust in thee." (Ps 56:3) The Risen Lord says, " Fear none of those things .... and I will give thee a crown of life." (2: 10)

(a) THE PRIZE THE RISEN LORD OFFERS:

The city of Smyrna was often called " the crown of Asia." Here the Lord Jesus offers the Christians of Smyrna an even better crown, the crown of life, which awaits them after death. A special crown, awaits all those who pay the ultimate price to be a follower of the Lamb.

(b) THE PROMISE THE RISEN LORD MAKES:

" He that overcometh shall not be hurt of the second death." (2:11) Christians can face the first death without fear because the second death has no power over us. (20:14)

(c) THE PERSON THE RISEN LORD IS:

To the church that is under pressure,

(1) THE RISEN LORD IS THE LASTING ONE:

" The first and the last." (2:8) From eternity past to eternity future, the Lord Jesus has been, is, and will always be the eternal and infinite one. What kind of perspective does a suffering church need ? An eternal perspective ! Remember that Jesus Christ existed Before Time, that He Rules Over Time and that He Will Reign For All Time. What we suffer here is insignificant to the eternal glory that awaits us there.

(2) THE RISEN LORD IS THE LIVING ONE:

" Which was dead and is alive." (2:8) We live and die. Christ died and lived. The shadow of death was daily hanging over this little flock at Smyrna. So Christ stands before them and says

" I am the living one, I have robbed death of its sting, of its fear. I am the Lord of your departure, for I hold in my hand the keys of death."

The Living Lord Jesus is in control of the Timing, Manner, and Place of death.

(3) THE RISEN LORD IS THE LOVING ONE:

He says, " I know." (2:9) That word know (oida) means the kind of knowledge that comes by personal experience. It also means to appreciate, respect, or value the worthiness of a person or thing. When Christ says, " I KNOW your tribulation," He is saying, " I know exactly what you're going through. I know because I've been there. I know what your tribulation feels like. I know what it is to be falsely accused, physically harmed, and spit upon. I know what you are suffering and I respect you greatly for it. I highly value your commitment to ME."

The Lord knew all about Polycarp the friend of the apostle John. In AD 155 at the age of 86, Polycarp, probably the leader of the church at Smyrna was summoned before the Roman proconsul. He was told to swear allegiance to Caesar and blaspheme Christ. He said, " Eighty and six years have I served the Lord Jesus. He has been faithful to me. How can I be faithless to Him, and blaspheme the name of my Saviour ?" Even threatened with death by wild beasts Polycarp remained true. Finally the Jews and Gentiles of Smyrna gathered wood on the Jewish Sabbath and used it to burn Polycarp alive.

There he stood by the stake asking not to be tied to it and he prayed, " O Lord I thank Thee that thou hast thought me worthy of this hour." He bowed his head and said " Amen," as the fires consumed him at the stake. Polycarp was faithful until death. When PERSECUTION hits the church, let us not fear the world .... but God and God alone. No matter what the cost.

Chapter Five

Living at Hell's Headquarters

❖

A special edition of Time Magazine, entitled, " Beyond The Year 2000, What To Expect In The Next Millennium," gives us a glimpse into the near future. As TIME'S editors and sociologists projected into the future, the view was not a very pretty one. What will our culture look like ? Where are we headed as a society? Now although this article was written primarily for the American public there is no doubt that the things that were spoken of us will affect us in the United Kingdom as well. Here is the picture.

(1) MULTIPLE MARRIAGES: "The family as we know it will soon die," they predicted. Replacing it will be marriages, or what will soon be "serial monogamy."

(2) WIDESPREAD DIVORCE: "Divorce will be so common as to be considered normal."

(3) WOMEN LIVING TOGETHER: "Many women will live with other women."

(4) MULTIPLE PARENTS: "Children will live with a bewildering array of relatives .... mothers, fathers, multiple stepmothers, multiple stepfathers etc."

(5) INCEST: "The taboo against incest will weaken. The fractured family will consist of relatives, non-relatives and former relatives, breaking down the obsolete prohibition against intimacies at home."

(6) CHILDLESSNESS: "The trend toward childlessness will accelerate. There will be more older people and fewer children than ever before."

(7) CHILD ABUSE: "Children will be routinely victimized and will be bounced from home to home as families splinter and reform and splinter and reform."

(8) SEXUAL EXPLOSION: "Pediatricians will teach children about the use of family planning at the time of their vaccinations against disease."

(9) ATHEISM: "Theology, the study of God and the Bible will soon die."

(10) FEMINISM: "The triumph of feminist religion will cause many to shun references to God in personal masculine terms. No more Heavenly Father."

(11) ABORTION:

Now this is what these socialists see in the future. Not a pretty picture. Begin with multiple marriages, divorce and lesbianism. Throw in incest, childlessness, and child abuse. Add sexual promiscuity, and abortion. Stir well with atheism. That is the world in which we will find ourselves. So says Time Magazine. And those editors may be right which is cause for concern. Undoubtedly, we have entered an era in which the culture is becoming increasingly hostile to Biblical values and morality. We are now living at hell's headquarters. We have set up church at the gates of hell. How should we then live ? What should be the church's strategy ? What counsel does Christ have to offer ? Now, more than ever, we must hear what Christ said to a little church in Pergamum.

It was a church that lived at hell's headquarters. They occupied the same neighbourhood as the devil. They served under the dark shadow of Satan's throne. Pergamum as the Greeks called it wasn't an easy place to live, yet that's where

God planted this church. Pergamos was situated about 55 miles north of Smyrna.

It was RENOWNED FOR ITS LIBRARY: it had one of the most famous libraries in the world. The library grew to 200,000 volumes before it was shipped to Egypt by Cleopatra. It was RESPECTED FOR ITS AUTHORITY: it was the capital city of the Roman province of Asia Minor. Here the Roman Governor had his seat of residence and he was the one man who had what the Romans called, "the power of the sword of life and death." It was REMEMBERED FOR ITS IDOLATRY: A 1,000 foot high hill overlooked the city and was covered with pagan temples, shrines and altars. Zeus, Athena, Dionysious and Asclepias each had temples built there. A huge altar to Zeus, the greatest of all Greek deities, had been built there in the form of a throne.

Moreover, Emperor worship had its strongest grip here. So deeply entrenched in idolatry was Pergamos that they had their own god named Asclepias, the god of healing. Worshippers would come into the temple of Asclepias to be healed. Snakes roamed wild throughout the temple. Worshippers were encouraged to lie down on the floor and allow these snakes to crawl over their body. Healing power was believed to be in the touch of these vipers. In fact do you know what the symbol of the medical profession is? A twisted serpent, which represents this god of healing, Asclepias. Now here is where this church found itself. Living at hells headquarters. Serving next to Satan's throne. Here is divine instruction which is most timely for our generation given the drift of our culture toward greater godlessness.

(1) THE FAITHFUL SAINTS

The Risen Lord begins with a word of encouragement. "I know." (2:13) Christ is saying, " I know exactly where you're living. I know what you're going through. I've been there. And I highly respect and value your faith in Me." The Risen

Lord knew what living at hell's headquarters meant. From the time of His birth, Satan began nipping at His heels. After forty days and forty nights in the wilderness, the Lord Jesus fought Satan head to head. All the artillery of hell was levelled at Christ. All the way to the cross, the Devil opposed and stirred up persecution against Christ. Now the Risen Lord says to the church at Pergamos, " I know."

(a) CHRIST KNEW ALL ABOUT THEIR LOCATION:

He says, " I know .... even where Satan's seat is." (2:13) That word " seat," is throne. Satan had his throne in Pergamos. The Devil is not Omnipresent. As a created being he can be in only one place at a time. He is " the prince of the power of the air," (Eph 2:2) and as such no doubt he has a throne somewhere in the heavenlies. He is also " the prince of this world," (John 12:31) and as such he has a throne somewhere on earth. In John's day it was at Pergamos ! " Satan's throne," means the place where his evil authority is most exercised. Now why was Pergamos, " Satan's throne "?

(1) A huge altar to Zeus, the greatest of all the Greek deities had been built there in the form of a throne. Many Bible scholars feel that, " Satan's throne," refers to this. Certainly at that time, this was the most famous pagan altar in the world.

(2) Pergamos was the centre of worship of Asclepias, the snake god. Here they worshipped in a great pagan temple with many snakes crawling inside the temple. Of course, all such superstitious idolatry was demonic.

(3) Pergamos was the regional centre of Emperor Worship. In other cities the citizens gave public testimony to Caesar's deity once a year. But here, a pinch of incense burned in worship of the Emperor was an every day occurrence.

The word " dwellest," is interesting. When the New Testament speaks of a Christian " dwelling," anywhere in this world it uses a Greek word (paroikein) which describes a temporary Residence in contrast with a permanent Residence.

This word is used of a " stranger and pilgrim." But that is not the word that is used here. (katoikein) The word that is used here speaks of, " residence in a permanent and settled place." What Christ is saying to these believers is, " You're living at hell's headquarters and you have to go on living there, you cannot pack your bags and move off to some other place where it is easier to be a Christian. In Pergamos you ARE, in Pergamos you MUST STAY."

(b) CHRIST KNEW ALL ABOUT THEIR LOYALTY:

They were living at hell's headquarters and that meant they had to be faithful and they were. They had been tempted to give in but they had stood firm. They were loyal to the PERSON OF CHRIST: " thou holdest fast my name." (2:13) His name stands for Himself. It is the revelation of Who Christ is and What Christ has done. It represents the Fullness of his Divine Human Person and Saving work. In a city where there was much to prise them loose they had firmly held to the conviction that Christ is both LORD and SAVIOUR and they never let go.

They were loyal TO THE PRECEPTS OF CHRIST: "And hast not my faith." (2:13) They would not deny His VIRGIN BIRTH: HIS VIRTUOUS LIFE: HIS VICARIOUS DEATH: HIS VICTORIOUS RESURRECTION: HIS VISIBLE RETURN. In the midst of a city which proclaimed FALSE GODS, they declared THE TRUE GOD. The cry of the citizens of Pergamos was, "ASCLEPIAS IS THE SAVIOUR," but the cry of the saints was, "JESUS IS SAVIOUR."

(c) CHRIST KNEW ALL ABOUT THEIR LOSS:

"Even in those days wherein Antipas was my faithful martyr." (2:13) The name Antipas means "against all," and that's precisely what he did. In his defence of the faith, he stood against all. This one man maybe the pastor of the church refused to yield to the " political correctness," of the day. Christ said, Antipas is " my faithful martyr." It cost him dearly. He "was slain among you, where Satan dwelleth." (2:13) Legend tells us that he was killed by being roasted to death in a brazen bull. A wise Christian knows which battles are worth fighting. A faithful Christian will do so.

(2) THE FLAGRANT SIN

Despite their steadfastness, sin had slipped in undetected. Their real danger was not with PERSECUTION FROM WITH-OUT, but it was from PERVERSION FROM WITHIN. If Satan can't defeat a church he'll join it. Error had crept in and the Risen Lord was concerned for the truth. The Risen Lord LOVES THE TRUTH: SPEAKS THE TRUTH: HE IS THE TRUTH: (John 8:31 14:6 18: 37) It seems at Pergamos most were continuing to walk in the truth but some had wandered into the by-path of error and the CHIEF SHEPHERD was grieved both by the WAYWARDNESS OF THE MINORITY and the INDIFFERENCE OF THE MAJORITY. What was this SIN about ?

(a) DOCTRINAL IN ITS ESSENCE:

Some were holding the " doctrine of Balaam." (2:14) The New Testament refers to Balaam on three occassions. It speaks of:

(1) THE WAY OF BALAAM: (2 Pet 2:15) His way was covetousness. Balaam's services could be readily bought.

(2) THE ERROR OF BALAAM: (Jude 11) He wrongly supposed that a Holy God would be forced to curse sinful Israel.

(3) THE DOCTRINE OF BALAAM: (2:14) He rightly concluded that if you cannot CURSE THEM, then CORRUPT THEM through Idolatry and Immorality. Who was Balaam? What did he teach ? During the time of Israel's wilderness wanderings, God's chosen people defeated the Ammonites, and Moab looked to be the next to fall. When Balak, the King

of Moab received a report that the Israelites were advancing his way, he knew there was no way his army could defeat Israel. In desperation Balak called on Balaam for help. The King said, " I've got a job for you. I want you to curse these people. And I'll make it worth your while." So Balaam sold his gift for profit.

Three times he tried to curse the people of God. But each time only blessings .... not cursings came out. (Num 22-24) So he devised an ingenious plan. If he could not Curse them, his only hope was to get GOD to do so. So he hatched a plot. The plot was WOMEN. (Num 25:1-3) The word "stumblingblock " (skandalon) (2:14) is interesting. It means a trap set with a bait. Balaam instructed Balek to place sensuous women before the marching Israelite army. He did and they wilted. Before they knew they lay down with dogs and got up with the devil's fleas. Soon they went to church with these heathen women and worshipped their idols. The result? God slew 24,000 Israelite men.

The teaching of Balaam IS TO COMPROMISE WITH THE WORLD. It is the mixing of holy things with unholy things. It is having one foot in the church and one foot in the world. This small group in Pergamos was threatening to destroy the whole church. In addition, the Risen Lord addresses another dangerous sin. " The doctrine of the Nicolaitanes." (2:15) Scholars are divided as to what this was. Some think it was an immoral teaching. Others feel it was the beginning of the distinction between clergy and laity. The teaching of Balaam encouraged believers to engage in IDOLATRY AND IM-MORALITY.

John says, " Little children, keep yourselves from idols." (1 John 5:2) Immorality is (porneia) That is an all-encompassing word that includes all forms of sexual perversions. Adultery. Premarital sex. Homosexuality. Lesbianism. Pornography. Common-law living together. The whole stinking mess. This is the IMMORAL teaching of Balaam. God's Word has not changed one bit. " Thou shalt NOT commit adultery." (Exod 20:14) " Flee fornication." (1 Cor 6:18) " For this is the will of God even your sanctification." (1 Thes 4:3) "But fornication and all uncleaness let it not be once named among you, as becometh saints." (Eph 5:3) The Risen Lord says, " There's a small group in your church that is teaching compromise with the world, DEAL WITH IT."

(b) SATANICAL IN ITS SOURCE:

The source of this error was Satan. Satan's throne was at Pergamos. The implication is clear. Satan was the SOURCE of the errors to which some of these people had succumbed. The Devil hadn't been able to DESTROY them by coming as THE ROARING LION (Antipas was proof of that) so he DECEIVED them through false teaching. Someone has said, " There are two means by which the influence of the church may be defeated and her distinctions obliterated. The one is PERSECUTION, the other is AMALGAMATION. The World may DESTROY the church by slaying its members or by making them worldlings."

(c) PROPHETICAL IN ITS OUTLOOK:

We can look at the churches Prophetically (1:3) and Pergamos suggests to us that period between 315-590 AD. Pergamos means "MARRIAGE." And then the church and state were wedded together. One of the key individuals during this period was Constantine. He was made Emperor in 306 AD by his dying father and the Roman troops. In 313 AD he signed the edict of TOLERATION which granted freedom to Christians.

It then became fashionable to join the church. He promised gold pieces and white robes to all converts. Soon pagans had joined the church by thousands bringing with them their heathen practices. The church then became so WORLDLY and the world so CHURCHY that no difference could be seen. It was during this time that many unscriptural doctrines were introduced.

(1) SAYING PRAYERS FOR THE DEAD: (300)
(2) MAKING THE SIGN OF THE CROSS: (300)
(3) THE WORSHIP OF SAINTS AND ANGELS: (375)
(4) THE INSTITUTION OF THE MASS: (394)
(5) THE WORSHIP OF MARY: (431)
(6) THE DOCTRINE OF PURGATORY: (593)

During this period in the church's history the world infiltrated the church and the church became wedded to the world.

(3) THE FINAL SUMMONS

(a) TO EXERCISE DISCIPLINE:

The entire church is called upon here to " repent," either of holding to this heresy or of allowing it to be spread. The Risen Lord does not say, " It is okay. I've got unlimited grace and unending forgiveness, so it doesn't matter how you live."

Christ says, " Repent or else." (2:16) His Coming here is not the RAPTURE. He's talking about a RUPTURE . This is a threat. A warning to heed. This does not refer to His Second Coming, but to a special coming in judgment to this particular church. Such a judgment fell on Balaam (Num 22:23 31 25:5 31:8) And such a severe discipline will come against the Balaamites in this church. The church must deal with sin, or Christ will come and deal with the church. We are to be GUARDIANS OF THE TRUTH. We are to maintain the PURITY OF THE CHURCH and how are we to do that? " With the sword of His mouth." The Word of God.

(b) TO EXPERIENCE BLESSING:

" To him that overcometh will I give to eat of the hidden manna and will give him a white stone, and in the stone a new name written, which no man knoweth saving he that receiveth it." (2:17) That is to all who withstand false doctrine and walk uncompromisingly in God's sight, the Risen

Lord promises three things. Hidden manna: a white stone: and a new name.

HIDDEN MANNA: Christ is the true manna, the living bread that comes down from above (John 6:35) This speaks of our fellowship with Him. Here believers are promised sweet communion with Christ forever.

A WHITE STONE: White stones were often given in the first century as a symbol of appreciation and acceptance, or specifically as a means of admission to a special event. Christ promises all true believers that in overcoming, they will be rewarded with eternal acceptance and admission into His presence.

A NEW NAME: A new name indicates a new identity. A new standing. It reflects a believer's new status in Christ. These three all fit together. One day each of us will be accepted (the white stone) into the presence of Christ to enjoy sweet fellowship (the hidden manna) according to our new status in Christ. (the new name)

(c) TO EXPOUND TRUTH:

This is the theme of this letter. The Risen Lord is deeply concerned that the truth be PRESERVED and PROCLAIMED. He reveals Himself to this church as, " He which hath the sharp sword with two edges." (2:12) In Roman culture a sword was the symbol of power and authority. In that day Rome had the power of the sword. Whatever Caesar determined became the law of the land. And he backed it up with the sword. Here the Lord Jesus is pictured as the unrivalled Lord of His church with power over life and death. His word is final. His law is binding. His rule is absolute.

This church was tolerating false teachers and they needed to be reminded that there is an unchanging standard .... the two-edged sword .... the Word of God by which God measures all truth. They must DEFEND and DECLARE sound doctrine. The Risen Lord loves the TRUTH. How then can we be indifferent to it ?

Chapter Six

A Devil with a Skirt On

❖

If there is a watchword that describes the Western mind-set today it is the word tolerance. Many folk in the Western world worship at the shrine of tolerance. In the shaping of public opinion and the forging of national policy, many esteem the broadmindedness which says any and all values, if sincerely held, are equally valid. There are no absolutes today. The only absolute is that there are not absolutes. Many people tolerate everything except intolerance.

Webster, defines the word tolerance like this: "the allowable deviation from a standard: sympathy or indulgence for beliefs or practices differing or conflicting with one's own." That, in a nutshell is the Western World. An openness that embraces almost ANYTHING morally, politically or educationally. George Gallop, America's pollster, says that 67 percent of Americans today believe that there is no such thing as absolute truth. In other words, right and wrong varies from situation to situation. It may be wrong for me, but right for you. Translated, if homosexuality is right for you, that's fine. If it's not right for you, well that's fine, too. Whatever works for you is right for you. If it feels good, do it. The consequences are terrifying. In USA Newsweek, in its December 7th 1992 issue, published an article entitled, "What Traditional Family?" The article referred to traditional values as a "myth," that never existed in American life. Interpreted, "we're rewriting history in order to be politically correct." In America and throughout Western Society, there is a growing and emerging belief that there is no absolute truth. No standard of right and wrong. The result is tolerance of any and every belief in our culture."

Like ancient Israel, we have become a people who have forgotten how to blush. Nothing shocks us anymore. Tragically we have become desensitized toward sin. In the name of tolerance, we have now opened the floodgates to embrace every form of wickedness. All people want is tolerance. An absolute standard of right and wrong is becoming a dusty page of ancient history. Who is to say which abnormal perversion will be accepted next ? Will it be polygamy ? Or child pornography ? Will it be transvestitism ? What " alternative lifestyle," will be next to be embraced ?

As the church we are beginning to feel the tightening noose of the world around us. If we are not careful we'll soon be choked to death by public consensus. Paul warns us, " Be not conformed to this world .... " (Rom 12:2) Now this was the tightening squeeze that the church at Thyatira felt .... the crunch of remaining intolerant in a tolerant society. Sadly, the world was influencing this church more than they were influencing the world. The Risen Lord must forcibly address this church. He must tell them that He is intolerant of that which they tolerate. There was a woman in their congregation, Jezebel, who was dressed to kill. She was A DEVIL WITH A SKIRT ON. The church is still being confronted with devil's wearing skirts who seek to lure and seduce the church. But God's standard of truth never changes. " The grass withereth, the flower fadeth but the Word of our God shall stand forever." (Is 40:8)

GEOGRAPHICALLY: Thyatira was located about 30 miles southeast of Pergamos. Of the seven cities this was the smallest. It was a small industrial centre between Pergamos and Laodicea. It was out of the way. The least known. The most obscure. Thyatira was a sentinel military town. It was originally settled to intercept any foreign armies approaching Pergamos. Before an invading foe could threaten the capital city, Pergamos, it had to defeat Thyatira first.

COMMERCIALLY: the city was prospering. In many ways, modern Thyatira, the Turkish city of Akhisar is much like it was in the days of the apostle John. Akhisar is still a busy commercial centre, and even in the 1990's its most important exports are essentially the same products that ancient Thyatira was known for: cotton and wool cloth, fruits and dyes. It is was from Thyatira, that Lydia the seller of purple came. (Acts 16:14)

Thyatira was in a city in which trade unions were very important. There were for example associations for bakers: bronze-workers: cobblers: weavers: tanners or dyers potters etc.; and if you wanted to prosper in business in Thyatira you had to be a " card-carrying," member. This is where the real problem for the believers came in. Each of these trade guilds had its own pagan deity. After hours the members were expected to attend the guild festivals. These included a feast of eating food offered to their idol and plunging into the vilest sexual orgies. Could a Christian participate in all of this ? If you did then you ensured your material prosperity, if you refused you ensured your material poverty.

What Jezebel was doing was this. She was using her powers of persuasion to encourage the fellowship to participate in pagan feasts and sexual promiscuity. No wonder our Risen Lord speaks to this fellowship in such a stern way.

(1) THE RISEN LORD PRAISES THEIR STRENGTHS

There are definite virtues for which Christ can praise them. This church had a lot going for it. Love, faith, service, and perseverence marked this congregation. These four virtues are actually two couplets. Their love led to their service and their faith produced perseverance.

(a) LOVE AND SERVICE:

Another translation reads, " I know your works, namely your charity and service and faith and patient endurance and that your recent works are more numerous and greater than your first ones." (2:19) While love for Christ was decreasing in Ephesus, it was increasing in Thyatira. This church remained deeply in love with Christ. In a day of callous indifference their devotion to Christ grew stronger and stronger.

Many years ago Thomas K. Beecher once substituted for his famous brother, Henry Ward Beecher, at the Plymouth Church in Brooklyn, New York. Many curiosity-seekers had come to hear the renowned Henry Beecher. But when Thomas Beecher appeared in the pulpit instead, some people got up and started for the doors. They were sadly disappointed to miss the opportunity to hear the famed orator speak. Sensing their disappointment because he was substituting for his brother, Thomas raised his hand for silence. He then announced, " All those who came here this morning to hear Henry Ward Beecher may withdraw from the church. All who came to worship God may remain."

Love for Christ not for any man must always be central in the church. Their love for God produced SERVICE. Love must be our divine motivation to serve others. They were constantly reaching out to minister to the needs of others. They gave themselves tirelessly to one another. Dwight L. Moody once said, "The measure of a man is not how many servants he has, but how many servants he serves."

(b) FAITH AND PATIENCE:

They trusted God to guide and provide. They relied upon Him to meet their needs. They were committed to following

Christ. Their Faith produced Perseverance. Perseverance (hupomone) is a steadfast endurance that bears up under great stress and mounting pressures. Their faith kept them faithful to complete the task to which Christ had called them. What's more, their love, service, faith and perseverance were increasing. Christ noted, " Your recent works are more numerous and greater than your first ones." They weren't stagnant, but growing in each of these areas.

(2) THE RISEN LORD PERCEIVES THEIR SIN

When Oliver Cromwell sat for the official portrait that would portray his appearance to future generations, he instructed the artist to paint just as he was. He wanted no flattery. In Cromwell's words he instructed the artist to paint him, "warts and all." As Christ paints the picture of this church, He does so warts and all. Shifting gears, the Lord says, "Notwithstanding I have a few things against thee because thou sufferest that woman Jezebel .... " (2:20)

They had a big problem in Thyatira and it could be summed up in one word, JEZEBEL. Their sin was, they tolerated her false teaching in the church. This church had love but no sound doctrine. Ephesus was just the opposite. They had sound doctrine but no love. Now a church will usually be polarised in one or the other direction. Either they will have full heads and empty hearts, or full hearts and empty heads. And either polarization is deadly. Balance is the key in the church. God demands both love and sound doctrine. We must " speak the truth in love." (Eph 4:15) The church at Thyatira had gotten out of balance.

They had all love but no doctrine. The result was devastating. Their lack of sound doctrine made this fellowship easy prey for the false teaching of a woman in their congregation whom Christ calls JEZEBEL. Let's meet JEZEBEL and the sin she promoted.

(a) THIS SIN IS ENUNCIATED:

Christ is specific, " that woman JEZEBEL." (2:20) Who was JEZEBEL ?

(1) THE OLD TESTAMENT CHARACTER:

HER HISTORY: is brought before us in (1 Kings 16:31) She was a foreigner. Her father Ethbaal was a priest of Ashtaroth the Phoenician equivalent of the Greek goddess Aphrodite and the Roman Venus. HER IDOLATRY: is brought before us in (1 Kings 16:32) When she moved to Israel she brought her pagan idolatry with her. The worship of Baal, the pagan fertility god, included the grossest sexual immoralities imaginable. The temples of Baal were filled with temple prostitutes, both male and female, and the basest sexual practices. According to one source JEZEBEL means pure and chaste but she contradicted HER NAME by HER NATURE.

HER MINISTRY: was TO CONTAMINATE: (2 Kings 9:22) Like Balaam before her she sought to contaminate Israel and her hen-pecked husband Ahab, lacked the courage to withstand her. TO DOMINATE: She was manipulatively dominant. She had Naboth killed. (1 Kings 21) And although Ahab was the king, Jezebel ran the country through her husband. She was the puppeteer behind the scenes, pulling the strings and setting the agenda in Israel. In truth, she was A DEVIL WITH A SKIRT ON. Her MINISTRY was to Contaminate, to Dominate, and also TO ERADICATE: (1 Kings 18:4) Ruthless. Godless. Calculating. Scheming. Power-mad. A seducer of people. Ahab was the figurehead, she was the sovereign head. But back to Thyatira. Come from this Old Testament Character:

(2) THE NEW TESTAMENT COUNTERPART:

There is a woman in this church just like JEZEBEL. HER HISTORY: is brought before us, " that woman Jezebel." (2:20) Some render the phrase, " thy woman Jezebel," or " thy wife Jezebel." Now if that's correct the inference is that this woman is the wife of the pastor/teacher or presiding elder. Others have said that Jezebel was Lydia. What we can say is this, Jezebel was a real woman in this church fellowship who claimed to have the gift of prophecy.

HER IDOLATRY: is brought before us "to teach and to seduce my servants to commit fornication, and to eat things sacrificed to idols." (2:20) Trade unions were very active in Thyatira. The men would work together all day, and then party all night. They would bring out their little pagan gods and start their idolatry. Prostitutes were involved as well. What were these believers to do ? Obviously, it was wrong to participate in this wickedness and yet because of the economic pressures, they would be out of work if they didn't.

HER MINISTRY: is brought before us " to teach and to seduce my servants to commit fornication, and to eat things sacrificed to idols." (2: 20) What was Jezebel's MINISTRY in this church ?

TO CONTAMINATE: " To teach .... my servants to commit fornication." (2:20) Jezebel was teaching them to join the unions. She said, " An idol is nothing. Go ahead and get involved in the guild. Participating in an meal won't hurt. God will overlook it. Business is business."

TO DOMINATE: The Risen Lord says, " Thou sufferest that woman to teach ...." (2:20) They had allowed her to occupy a teaching role.

TO ERADICATE: To root out the doctrine of separation and advocate compromise with the world for financial success. This false prophetess was actually teaching " the deep things of Satan." (2:24) She taught that you can't overcome evil until you all know all about it and even try it. Unfortunately many were buying into this and were being led astray. God's unchanging requirement is " Come out from among them, and be ye separate, saith the Lord." (2 Cor 6:17)

(b) THIS SIN IS TOLERATED:

The Risen Lord says, " thou sufferest that woman .... to teach." (2:20) The church at Thyatira believed in peaceful coexistence. " Don't rock the boat, don't say anything that would hurt her feelings." They were more concerned in pleasing her than pleasing the Lord. And Christ says: " I have a few things against thee." (2:20) What had the Risen Lord against them ? This, they tolerated a woman to reach an unscriptural position and teach an unscriptural doctrine. The New Testament is clear on this. Paul says, " But I suffer not a woman to teach, nor to usurp authority over the man but to be in silence." (1 Tim 2:12-14 1 Cor 14:34)

(c) THIS SIN IS REITERATED:

History repeats itself and when we look at this church prophetically (1:3) as representing a definite phase in history we come across some things that are most interesting. Thyatira represents that period from 590-1517 AD The name Thyatira means "Continual Sacrifice," and may refer in general to the Roman Catholic Church. For not long after the reign of Constantine ROME became the centre of church affairs and the DARK AGES of Church History began. Just as JEZEBEL introduced the abominations of Baal worship into Israel, so ROME incorporated Paganism into Christianity.

Consider The Papacy. ITS HISTORY: The word Pope means FATHER. At first it was applied to all Western Bishops but about 500 AD it began to be restricted to the Bishop of Rome. Gregory the 1st (590-694) was the first real pope. Other evil popes during this time were Sergius the 3rd (904-911) he lived with a harlot, Marozia and they raised their illegitimate children to become popes and cardinals. Benedict the 9th (1033-1045) was made Pope as a boy of 12 years of age. He committed murders and adulteries in broad daylight and robbed graves. Finally the enraged people of Rome drove him out of the city.

Consider The Papacy. ITS IDOLATRY: Idolatry is the worship of idols, strictly forbidden in the second commandment. (Exod 20:4-5) The Risen Lord identifies Himself to this church as " the Son of God." (2:18) Why ? Because Rome has accustomed people to think of Him as " the son of Mary," a position that robs Him of His essential Deity and thereby degrades HIM. Roman Catholics say, " I go to Mary and ask her to speak to Him on my behalf." The Bible says, " There is one God and one Mediator between God and men the man Christ Jesus." (1 Tim 2:5)

Consider The Papacy. ITS MINISTRY: What is its Ministry?

TO CONTAMINATE: The infidel historian Gibbon says this about this period. " The history of the church is the annals of hell." The church became the home of heathendom. Pagan feast days became Christian festivals. Pagan gods became Christian saints. Pagan priests became the ordained servants of the church.

TO DOMINATE: During this period God had his Elijahs. John Huss (1369-1415) was a fearless preacher who honoured the Bible above the church, he was burnt at the stake by the Pope. Rome has not changed Her Ministry, to Contaminate, to Dominate, and to Eradicate.

Some foolish Protestants are now saying, " Well, we never understood Rome, it is a pity we had the Reformation at all." Have they forgotten the millions of lives that were sacrificed because they stood for the truth ? Have they forgotten the cry of the Reformation? " By Grace alone, Through faith alone, in Christ alone."

(3) THE RISEN LORD PRONOUNCES THEIR SUFFERING

If the church at Thyatira was not going to deal with this sin the Risen Lord was for He threatens the direst judgments. There is an unbreakable law in God's moral universe of sowing and reaping. We always reap what we sow. If we sow sin we will surely reap suffering. It's the law of the harvest.

Consequently, Christ promised: "And I gave her space to repent of her fornication and she repented not. Behold, I will cast her into a bed, and them that commit adultery with her into great tribulation, except they repent of her deeds. And I will kill her children with death: and all the churches shall know that I am he which searcheth the reins and hearts: and I will give unto every one of you according to your works." (2:21-23)

(a) THE LORD IS PATIENT IN JUDGMENT:

Jesus said, " I gave her time to repent." (2:21) God had already rebuked her for this false teaching. But despite having ample time to repent she REFUSED. She did not want to repent of her immorality. She likes her sin. She will not give it up.

(b) THE LORD IS PRECISE IN JUDGMENT:

" Behold I will kill her children with death." (2:22-23) The Amplified New Testament says, "I will throw her on a bed of anguish, or suffering." The suffering Christ refers to may be well be a reference to sexually transmitted diseases. Gonorrhea and syphilis were common in the ancient world. Sow to the flesh, reap to the flesh. Sexual promiscuity has a payday some-day. Every kick has a kickback. Solomon wrote, "Can a man take fire in his bosom, and his clothes not be burned?" (Prov 6:27) Play with fire and you'll get fire. Christ promised, "I will kill her children (followers) with death." (2:23) Would God kill a believer ? Would God put to death one of His own children ?

Yes. Christ is saying, " If YOU won't discipline her and her followers, then I will. It will be a discipline unto death." A believer can go too far into sin and commit a sin unto death. (Acts 5:1, 1 Cor 11:17, 1 John 5:16) Christ tells us why He takes such action.

(c) THE LORD IS PRACTICAL IN JUDGMENT:

He does this so that "all the churches shall know that I am He which searcheth the reins and hearts." (2:23) Christ wants other churches to know that He is serious about HOLINESS in the church. In other words Christ is saying, "I've got to discipline Thyatira because Ephesus is watching. I can't let this go unchecked because Smyrna is watching. I must deal with this sin because Pergamos is watching. If I don't judge Thyatira, then Ephesus, Smyrna, and Pergamos will begin to live like this."

There are too many sinning saints who are going unchecked in churches today. That's sending the wrong signal to other Christians that immorality is all right. He now speaks to the rest .... the faithful remnant who have not become entangled in this evil woman's teaching. And,

(4) THE RISEN LORD PROMISES
THEIR SUCCESS

(a) THE PERSON OF THIS PROMISE:

Who is HE ? He is the OMNISCIENT LORD. He has "eyes like unto a flame of fire." (2:18) With omniscient gaze Christ is able to see into the secret place of our hearts. He sees what no one else can see. He evaluates our inner motivations. He weighs our driving ambitions. He observes our secret thoughts. Everything is laid bare before Him. Nothing is hidden from His glowing eyes. Nothing. (Heb 4:13)

Who is HE ? He is the OMNIPOTENT LORD. " His feet are like fine brass." (2:18) With blazing feet He stands strong in judgment over this church. If " His eyes," are able to DETECT SIN, then " His feet," are able to DESTROY SIN. Why does Christ reveal Himself THIS way to THIS church? Because they have become tolerant of sin. And Christ will not tolerate a church married to the world.

(b) THE PEOPLE OF THIS PROMISE:

"But unto you I say, and unto the rest in Thyatira, as many as have not this doctrine, and which have not known the depths of Satan, as they speak: I will put upon you none other burden. But that which ye have already hold fast till I come." (2:24-25) Christ places no OTHER burden on these believers. But what burden does He give them ? The burden of having to bear with Mrs. JEZEBEL until something is done with her. In other words, " Just deal with her. That's all I want you to do. Just deal with her." In the meantime, " hold fast," to your purity: to your fidelity: to your integrity." Don't let go of what is right. Flee temptation and leave no forwarding address.

(c) THE PROSPECT OF THIS PROMISE:

Christ here (2: 26-28) quotes from (Ps 2:8-9) That's a Messianic Psalm looking ahead to the Second Coming of Christ to destroy God's enemies. When Christ returns to this planet, He will establish His earthly Kingdom and in that day we will rule and reign with Him. (1 Cor 6:2) The Risen Lord promises believers " the morning star." (2:28)

Today we know the morning star as the planet Venus, second planet from the sun and the brightest object in the night sky. Depending on where it is in its orbital path, the morning star can be seen to rise as much as three hours before the sun. In the last Book of the Old Testament there is a prophecy regarding the Return of Christ in power and glory, " But unto you that fear my name shall the SUN of righteousness arise with healing in His wings." (Mal 4:2) When He returns visibly to the Earth Christ will be like the noonday sun breaking through the gloom of the dark night of the world.

But before the sun arises, the morning star will appear. Christ says later in this Book, " I am the bright and morning star." (22:16) There will be two stages of the appearance of the Lord Jesus. First He will appear as the morning star, coming for His own. Then, at a later period He will appear as the shining sun, coming in all His power and glory visible to all the world. The prospect of the Morning Star is the prospect of the Rapture. "Our gathering together unto HIM." (2 Thes 2: 1) What an amazing prospect awaits us. Whether we have died or still live when He returns for us, He will gather us together to be with HIM. "Forever with the Lord."

What way will Christ find us spiritually? Walking in Worldliness or walking in Holiness? God is serious about our HOLINESS. That's the message to Thyatira. Murray McCheyne's prayer was, "Lord make me as holy as it is possible for a saved sinner to be."

Chapter Seven

A Morgue with a Steeple

❖

Calvin Coolidge was America's thirtieth president. He was an extremely quiet and reserved man. When questioned, he rarely answered more than two or three words ... a tendency which earned him the nickname "Silent Cal". The public saw him as a stiff and emotionless man. In 1933, the radio airwaves crackled with the news of Coolidge's death. Columnist Dorothy Parker was in her office at The New Yorker when a colleague flung open the door and blurted, "Dotty, did you hear? Coolidge is dead."

Endowed with a very quick wit, she shot back, "How can they tell?"

As we stand under the hot glare of our Lord's letter to Sardis we have to look honestly within and ask ourselves, "Can anyone tell if we are alive or dad? Am I truly alive ... or do I just have a reputation, a name for being alive?" The Lord's words to the church at Sardis are blunt and strong, "Thou hast a name that thou livest, and art dead." (3:1)

How can you have a dead church? Especially if the living Lord indwells it? How can a congregation be dead if the life of God pulsates through that body? Tragically, many churches are DEAD. Like the rotting carcass of Lazarus, these church bodies have the foul stench of death upon them. They have the appearance of life, but they are actually dead. Their sanctuary is A MORGE WITH A STEEPLE. They are congregations of corpses. They have undertakers for ushers. Embalmers for elders. And morticians for ministers. Their pastor graduated from the Cemetery. The choir master is the local coroner. They sing, "Embalmed in Gilead."

May be we've attended a dead church like that. The sermon was DEAD. The worship was DEAD. The fellowship was DEAD. They lost vital signs years ago. DEAD. DORMANT. DULL. This was the church at Sardis. A church with a great reputation. But now? There is no life. No dynamic. No pulse. No heartbeat. This letter to the church at Sardis is one of the most severe of the seven. Its criticism is almost unrelieved. Its spiritual history like its civil history belonged to the past.

HISTORICALLY SARDIS WAS IMPORTANT: It had once been one of the greatest cities of the ancient world. Founded some seven centuries before the Coming of Christ, it had a long and rich history. As the capital of the ancient kingdom of Lydia, it had been one of the wealthiest cities of the world.

GEOGRAPHICALLY SARDIS WAS IMPREGNABLE: It was located on an almost inaccessible plateau. The acropolis of Sardis was some 1,500 feet above the valley floor. As such, the city was thought to be an impregnable fortress against military assault. This security bred a smug self-sufficiency. The citizens thought they were invincible against the invading armies. So, they ceased positioning their watchmen on the tower. But Cyrus, Kin g of the Medo-Persians, captured Sardis by scaling a secret path up the cliff below. Once conquered, the city fell into a downward spiral from which they never recovered. By the end of the first century the city was a mere shadow of its former glory.

COMMERCIALLY SARDIS WAS INDUSTRIOUS: The city lay about 50 miles east of Ephesus, at the junction of five roads, making it a centre for trade. The city was known for its manufacture of woollen garments and the main religion of the city was the worship of Artemis, one of the nature cults that was founded on the belief of death and rebirth.

MORALLY SARDIS WAS INDECENT: It was a name of contempt. Its people were loose-living and luxury loving. It was a city of decadence. This city had a name that it was living but it was dead. Now the church in Sardis had become like the city. Proud. Smug. Self-sufficient. Cruising on past momentum. Alive in name only. What a warning to all great churches that are living on past glory. Vance Havner reminds us that spiritual ministries often go through four stages. "A Man, A Movement, A Machine, and A Monument." Sardis was at the Monument stage, but still there was hope.

(1) A REPUTATION THAT WAS IMPRESSIVE

"Thou hast a NAME that thou livest." (3:1) Or as another translation renders it, "You have a reputation of being alive." This church had acquired a name: its reputation had spread far and wide. It was known by the other six churches in Asia Minor for its VITALITY. No false doctrine was taking root in this church. We don't hear of Balaam, or the Nicolaitanes or Jezebel in this church. This church had built up quiet an impressive reputation.

This was the place to be. It was highly revered and respected. No doubt they prided themselves on their illustrious past.

But that was the problem. They lived in the past. In the present they had only an empty, lifeless profession. Reputations are a funny thing. We care more about what we think people think about us than what they actually think about us. Someone has said that wen we turn twenty, we worry about what people think about us. When we turn forty, we stop worrying about what others think about us. When we turn sixty we realise that no one has been thinking about us at all.

Now this was the problem with the Sardis church. They so prided their reputation built up in the past that they lost all spiritual power in the present. They had built quite an impressive reputation but,

(a) INWARDLY THEY WERE DEAD

"Thou hast a name that thou livest, and are dead." (3:1) What does it mean, "Thou art dead"? It doesn't mean that they were spiritually lost. The Bible says that those without Christ are DEAD in trespasses and sins. (Ephesians 2:1). But this death at Sardis means that the spiritual vitality of the members was non-existent. This church was outwardly active. They had all the signs of dynamic ministry. But their inward condition was dead. They were living off yesterday's spiritual momentum. A cold, formal rigidness had set in. What does a dead church look like?

(1) **DEAD PREACHING:** In the pulpit, a mild-mannered man speaks to mild-mannered people, encouraging them to be more mild-mannered. He has eloquence, but no unction. He has proper diction, but no dynamic. He is like an old heater that has broken, the blower is still working but the heat is gone.

(2) **DEAD WORHSIP:** It's like walking into a wax museum. There's no excitement. No buzz. They worship as if the Lord Jesus was still dead and buried in the grave. They begin at 11:00 am SHARP and get out at 12:00 DULL.

(3) **DEAD MINISTRY:** There is no evangelism. No missions outreach. No church growth. Cobwebs are spun in the baptistry.

Oliver Cromwell was once faced with a shortage of precious metal for coins so he sent his troops out to find some. When they returned, they reported that the only precious metal was to be found in the statues of the saints standing in the corners of the churches. Cromwell said, "Well, melt the saints down and put them in circulation." Isn't this the problem with dead churches? The saints are no longer in circulation and need to be melted down.

(4) DEAD HOPE: All they do is live in the past. At the bottom of the church stationery they proudly display their church motto, "We've never done it that way before." They worship at the shrine of tradition. They live in the good old days. They don't have REVIVALS they have REUNIONS.

(b) SPIRITUALLY THEY WERE DEFICIENT

Christ says, "For I have not found thy works perfect before God." (3:2) The word "perfect" means "complete". It would seem that in Sardis they were STARTERS but not FINISHERS. They were many doing many things but completing none. Dwight L. Moody used to remark, "I would rather say, this one thing I do, than say these forty things I dabble with."

The church at Sardis was DABBLING instead of DOING. The Risen Lord could say, "I have not found thy works perfect before God." Their works measured up to man's standard but not to God's. Before God this church was the opposite of what she was before man. Men looked upon her works with DELIGHT, God looked upon her works with DISGUST.

(c) MORALLY THEY WERE DEFILED

The Risen Lord said, "Thou hast a few names even in Sardis which have not defiled their garments." (3:4) There is a faithful remnant here. There were a few people in Sardis who were still spiritually vibrant. This core group had abstained from moral impurity. They had not compromised with the world around them. They had not grown comfortable with the godless culture. They refused to soil their robes with the world's filth and because they had not yielded to temptation, the Lord promises to replace their human garments with specially prepared white robes. But the majority in Sardis were DEFILED. According to the Greek historian Herodotus, the citizens of Sardis had, over the course of many years, acquired a reputation for lax moral standards and even open licentiousness. Tragically this had permeated into the life of the fellowship and was detected by the Risen Lord. But while the vast majority in the church had been defiled here was a core group that had abstained from moral impurity.

(2) A REFORMATION THAT WAS IMPERATIVE

The problem with the church at Sardis was that she was DEAD but all was not lost for the Lord saw the glow of embers among the ashes and exhorted the believers, especially, I beleive, this godly remnant, (3:4) to fan the flame.

(a) SOUGHT IN THE SAINTS OF GOD

What did the Risen Lord say to this church of zombies?

1. BE WATCHFUL:

"Be watchful," or "Wake up." (3:2) In Greek these words are sharp, staccato commands. They are like a slap in the face, a splash of cold water, a sniff of ammonia. Christ is saying, "Come out of your spiritual hibernation. Arouse yourself." This almost impregnable city had twice fallen to surprise attacks. The first time to Cyrus (549 BC) the second time to Antiochus (218 BC). What had happened in the city happened in the church for is it not remarkable that Asia Minor (now Turkey) was once the brightest spot for Gospel witness, but today it is one of the darkest. The lampstand has been removed.

2. BE USEFUL:

"Strengthen the things which remain that are ready to die."
(3:2) This refers to the basics of the spiritual life ... Bible study;
prayer; worship and fellowship. Christ is saying, "Get back
into the Word. Get back into prayer. Get back into fellowship,.
Get back to the basics." Now the word, "strengthen" here was
often used in the Early Church for the nurture of believers.
(Acts 18:23) New Christians are weak. They need to be
strengthened: babies need to be nurtured: the unstable need
to be established.

3. BE MINDFUL:

"Remember therefore how thou hast received and heard"
(3:3) What had they received and heard at the beginning? The
gospel. They had received the basic truths of the Christian
life. This is not a call to live in the past, but a command to
remember their rich spiritual heritage in Christ. Christ is saying here, "Remember how you were saved! Remember how
you were nothing before God found you! Remember how
God's grace reached down and redeemed you." The Lord is
ever calling our wandering thoughts and affections back to
Himself. His last act before He went to Cavalry was to insti-
tute a FEAST OF REMEMBRANCE to draw us back to Himself again and again during our pilgrimage on earth.

4. BE HEEDFUL:

"Hold fast and repent." (3:3) Or "Remember the Word you
received and obey it." Here is Christ's appeal to obey God's
Word ... to keep His commandments ... in every area of their
lives. Disobedience and spiritual dryness are twin sisters.
Wherever you find one, you will be sure to find the other.
Christ is saying, "Weave God's truth through every area of
your life. Keep the Word. Put it into practice."

A husband and wife were discussing the possibility of taking a trip to the Holy Land. "Wouldn't it be fantastic to go to the Holy Land," he said, "and stand and shout the Ten Commandments from Mount Sinai?" "It would be better," his wife retorted pointedly, "if we stayed at home and kept them!" "Hold fast and repent." It means to let go of our sins. Obedience and Repentance.

(b) WROUGHT BY THE SPIRIT OF GOD

The way the Lord presents Himself to each church is a clue to what that particular church needs. Here we read, "These things saith he that hath the seven Spirits of God." (3:1) Who or what are the seven Spirits of God? The first occurrence of this phrase is found in (1:4-5) There "the seven Spirits" are linked with the Eternal Father and with Jesus Christ as the single source of both grace and peace. (4:5, 5:6) We conclude therefore that "the seven spirits" are the Holy Spirit. So when John records, "These things saith he that hath the seven Spirits of God," (3:1), he isn't saying that there are seven Holy Spirits, but that there is one perfect Holy Spirit and when the Spirit comes He comes in full and perfect power.

The Holy Spirit is the Spirit of LIFE (Rom 8:2, Isa. 11:3) What did the church at Sardis need? LIFE. It is the Spirit of God who can breath LIFE into our formal worship and make it living. It is the Spirit of God who can animate our "dead works" and make them pulsate with LIFE. It is "Not by might, nor by power, but by My Spirit, saith the Lord of Hosts" (Zech 4:6) But the Christ who "hath the seven Spirits of God," has also "the seven stars." (3:1)

Now, who are the seven stars? "The seven stars are the angels (messengers) of the seven churches." (1:20) "The seven stars," are in His right hand. (1:16, 2:1) Are "the seven Spirts of God," in His left? If only He would bring His hands together. If only the Holy Spirit would FILL/CONTROL the

MESSENGERS SPECIFICALLY and the BELIEVERS CONTINUALLY.

Now the word Sardis means, "a remnant", or "Those who have escaped." Prophetically it brings us to the period: 1517-1700. It brings before us the great state churches of the Reformation who escaped from Rome only to fall eventually into cold, lifeless formalism.

J. Vernon McGee writes: "This is a picture of Protestantism. The great truths which were recovered in the Reformation have been surrendered by a compromising church. Although the great denominations and churches still repeat by rote the creeds of the church, in mind, heart, and life they have repudiated them. Imposing programmes, elaborate rituals, and multiplication of organisations have been substituted for the Word of God and real spiritual life. There is activity but no actions: motion without movement: promotion without progress: programme without power. Although the outward form remains the living creature has vacated the shell."

In this period of church history God raised up His men. Martin Luther (1483-1546) after three miserable years in the priesthood he found peace with God. Then there was Zwingli (1484-1531) Luther's co-worker. Then there was John Calvin (1509-1564) one of the greatest theologians of the Christian faith. Then there was John Knox (1515-1572) who swept popery out of Scotland.

(3) A RECOGNITION THAT WAS INSTRUCTIVE

The Risen Lord says, "He that overcometh, the same shall be clothed in white raiment, and I will not blot out his name out of the book of life, but I will confess his name before my Father, and before His angels." (3:5) To be taken by the hand by the Lord Jesus, to be led up past the marshalled ranks of angels, up along the golden avenues of glory, up past the cherubim and seraphim, up, up to the throne of God Himself and to hear the Lord Jesus call you by your name and present you in person as His well beloved. Then to hear the Father say, "Bring the best robe and put it on him." That's RECOGNITION.

But this RECOGNITION is only possible:

(a) IF FELLOWSHIP IS REAL

Who will be clothed in white raiment? The overcomer. Who will walk with Christ in white? Those who have not defiled their garments. Those who do not DISGRACE THE GARMENTS OF GRACE will DON THE GARMENTS OF GLORY (Jude 23).

(b) IF CITIZENSHIP IS REAL

"And I will not blot his name out of the book of life." (3:5) Does this mean that it is possible to have your name blotted out of the book of life? Does this mean that a Christian can lose his salvation? Unquestionably, the Bible teaches the eternal security of the believer. Once saved, always saved. So what is Christ promising here?

In John's day a King kept an official register that contained all the names of its citizens. A name would be removed if one committed a crime against the state. Or a name would be blotted out if a citizen moved or if he died. The book contained the names of all true citizens who had not rebelled against the King. Conversely, the Lord Jesus will never blot our names out of His book. Indeed the passage should actually be rendered, "I will never: ever under any circumstances blot out your name from the book of life." We were chosen in Christ before the beginning of time and what is predestined before time is settled for all time.

(c) IF DISCPLESHIP IS REAL

"But I will confess his name before my Father and before his angels." (3:5) This is what Christ said during His earthly ministry, "Whosoever shall confess me before men him will I confess also before My Father which is in heaven" (Matt. 10:32, Luke 12:38) What an honour to hear the Saviour say,"Father He confessed Me, in a godless culture, I confess him before Thee." So this letter ends. There is no indication that this church as a whole would hear this call but there is always a remnant.

A man once came to Gypsy Smith, the well known English evangelist and asked him how to have REVIVAL.

Gypsy asked, "Do you have a place where you can pray?"
"Yes," was the reply.
"Then I'll tell you what you must do," said the evangelist.
"You go to that place and take a piece of chalk along. Kneel down there and with the chalk and draw a complete circle all around you. Then pray for God to send revival on everyone inside the circle. Stay there until He answers ... and you will have revival."

Chapter Eight

A Little Church with a Big God

❖

Certain men seem to rise above the landscape of their day and make a mark for Jesus Christ on their generation. Donald Gray Barnhouse was one of those spiritual giants. As the pastor of the Tenth Presbyterian Church of downtown Philadelphia, Pennsylvania, Dr. Barnhouse towered above his times and left an impact for eternity. Soon after graduating from Princeton Theological Seminary, Barnhouse was invited back to campus to preach. For a young pastor this was quite an intimidating experience. As Barnhouse stepped into the pulpit to address the student body and faculty, he was suddenly quite nervous. In attendance that day was one of the most brilliant men on the face of the earth .... an Old Testament professor named Dr. Robert Wilson.

Professor Wilson was a genius who reportedly read twenty seven languages and was highly respected for his proven scholarship in the Scriptures. As Barnhouse stood to speak, Dr. Wilson sat with arms folded on the front row, peering stoically over the top of his glasses. The young pastor preached the best he could, but he found it difficult not to be preoccupied with his famous professor seated so prominently at his feet. 'What is Dr. Wilson thinking?' Barnhouse wondered. 'Does he approve?' Then suddenly, a disturbing thing happened. Midway through Barnhouse's message, Professor Wilson shuffled his papers together. He stood to his feet and walked out of the church building while Barnhouse was still preaching. Barnhouse was crushed. What had he said to offend Dr. Wilson? Where had he failed? Was his theology wrong? What about his use of the original languages ? Barnhouse could barely gather the strength to finish his message.

After the ordeal was over, the young preacher exchanged a few plesantries with well-wishers and then went straight to the professor's office. He knocked on the door and with a trembling voice asked, ' Where did I fail ?' Dr. Wilson stopped his reading and looked up. ' Fail? Oh, you didn't fail,' Wilson explained. ' I always come to hear my former students speak one time. I simply want to know if they believe and preach in a big God or a small God. I am very pleased that you are one of our few graduates who believe and preach a big God. I didn't need to hear anymore.'

What a lesson for Barnhouse. What a lesson for us. Those who believe in a great God are those who do great things for God. He delights in taking ordinary people and doing extraordinary things through them. That way, the greatness belongs to Him.

The size of our God will determine the impact of our lives. Churches with a big God conduct extraordinary ministry. Those who believe and serve a great God shake this world for Jesus Christ ! Now this is what makes the Lord's letter to the church at Philadelphia so important. They ministered in one of the smallest of the seven cities, and yet the believers there had the greatest opportunity for ministry before them. Why? Because their eyes were upon a great God. There are several things about this city that we need to note for undoubtedly they have a bearing on the Lord's remarks here.

Consider ITS HISTORICAL BACKGROUND: It was founded by Attalus the Second in 140 BC and Attalus was called Philadelphos (brotherly love) It was after him that Philadelphia was named. Now Attalus had built this city for one main reason, that it might become a missionary city. It was intended that the function of Philadelphia was to spread the Greek culture, language and civilisation. What the city had been for Greek Culture, the church was to be for the Christian Gospel.

Consider ITS GEOGRAPHICAL LOCATION: The location of this city was significant. There are three important considerations in the sale of property, location, location, location. Philadelphia had all three. Because of its location 25 miles southeast of Sardis, this city was a major hub of communication, disseminating information throughout this part of the known world.

Ancient travellers would pass through Philadelphia on their way to important destinations. As the " Gateway to the East," it was ideally situated to touch the lives of many people. Beyond this small settlement lay the kingdoms of Lydia: Missia: and Phrygia. No doubt it was that Christ was thinking about when He said " I have set before .... an open door." (3:8) However, Philadelphia also sat on a geological fault that made the city vulnerable to volcanoes and earthquakes. In AD 17 this city was devastated. In the following years the city continued to be jolted by aftershocks. So much so that many of the residents moved out permanently to live in the surrounding fields for fear of being buried alive. The Risen Lord's promise to the overcomer was " He shall go no more out." (3:12)

Consider ITS SPIRITUAL CHURCH: This church was weak but it was wonderful. Like Smyrna there's no rebuke here. Nothing but praise is given. It was a Revival Church. It had experienced an EVANGELICAL REVIVAL: it had a world vision. It had experienced an ECCLESIASTICAL REVIVAL: the deadening influence of Judaism had been overcome. It had experienced an ESCHATOLOGICAL REVIVAL: The truth of the Lord's Return was its beacon light. Thus the Risen Lord stands before this fellowship not to offer blame, but blessing, not the threat of a fearful vengeance, but the thrill of a fresh vision.

In this letter there are three symbols: " A KEY " (3:7) " A DOOR," (3:8) " A PILLAR," (3:12) We want to examine the relationship between THE CHURCH'S OPEN DOOR: THE LORD'S MASTER KEY: AND THE OVERCOMER'S HEAVENLY PILLAR.

(1) THE OPPORTUNITY THAT LAY BEFORE THEM

" I have set before thee AN OPEN DOOR." (3:8) This is the first of 4 special doors in the Book of Revelation. There is: (1) The Door of the HUMAN HEART: (3:20) (2) The Door of the RAPTURE: (4:1) (3) The Door of the SECOND COMING: (19:11) (4) The Door of SERVICE: (3:8) An OPEN DOOR in Scripture is a door of OPPORTUNITY. Opportunity for service and ministry. An " open door," is a God-given opportunity for expanded ministry. Open doors lead to unlimited ministry potential for Christ. Open doors lead to vast new horizons.

(a) AN OPEN DOOR IS DIRECTED BY THE LORD:

" I have set .... open door." (3:8) Paul was aware of open doors divinely placed before him. The apostle writes, " For a great door and effectual is opened unto me." (1 Cor 16:9) Later he wrote, " When I came to Troas to preach Christ's gospel, and a door was opened unto me of the Lord." (2 Cor 2:12) Paul requested prayer " that God would open to us a door of utterance." (Col 4:3) Philadelphia was strategically placed. It was " The gateway to the East," ideally situated to touch the lives of many people and the Risen Lord says to this church, " I have .... open door." The opportunity to spread the good news of the gospel.

(b) AN OPEN DOOR IS EFFECTED BY THE CHURCH:

There is a cause and effect principle at work here. Another rendering of (3:8) reads " I have placed before you an open door that no one can shut BECAUSE you have a little power and have kept MY Word and not denied MY name." The Lord opened a door for this church BECAUSE this church had fulfilled certain conditions. They were faithful in little. So God gave them opportunity to be faithful in much.

(1) OUTWARDLY THEY WERE WEAK:

" Thou hast a little strength." (3:8) That may sound like a rebuke but it was not. It was merely a statement of fact. Compared to the other churches, they had only a little power. Limited resources, small numbers, and little clout. This was not a high-powered church. This was no well-oiled: high profile: hotly wired megachurch. They had no respected community leaders as their office-bearers. They lived from hand to mouth .... God's hand to their mouth. But it was in their weakness they learned a great lesson: faithfulness to God opens great doors. Even for the smallest churches.

(2) INWARDLY THEY WERE STRONG:

" Thou hast kept MY Word." (3:8) They were fiercely committed to God's Word. They preached it: taught it: believed it: obeyed it: lived it and shared it. They wouldn't budge from the Word. " And hast not denied My name." (3:8) Apparently many in Philadelphia, especially unbelieving Jews were persecuting the church. But this little band of believers would not buckle under worldly pressure. They remained true to the Lord who redeemed them. Boldly, they witnessed for Him in every opportunity. No wonder Christ opened doors for this

church. They were faithful in little so God gave them opportunity to be faithful in much.

(c) AN OPEN DOOR IS REJECTED BY THE WORLD:

Whenever, a church moves forward by faith it is sure to
meet the devil head-on. That's precisely what happened in
Philadelphia. The Lord notes, " Behold I will make them of
the synagogue of Satan, which say they are Jews, and are not,
but do lie: behold I will make them to come and worship
before thy feet, and to know that I have loved thee. Because
thou hast kept the word of my patience, I also will keep thee
from the hour of temptation, which shall come upon all the
world, to try them that dwell upon the earth." (3:9-10)

(1) THE FOE WAS POWERFULLY STRONG:

It was Jews who were causing trouble at Smyrna. (2:9)
They were at it again in Philadelphia. In this city there was a
group of Jews who met locally in a synagogue. They claimed
to be true sons of Abraham, but they weren't. They professed
faith in God, but they lied. They were unbelieving Jews, Satan
was their father. These Jews were persecuting the church,
slandering them and spreading vicious lies. And the Risen
Lord says, " I know .... " (3:8) The Saviour Himself had been
the target of Satan's synagogue during the days of His earthly
ministry. It was the religious Pharisees who levelled the greatest hatred against the Lord Jesus. Despite their claims to be
true sons of Abraham, Christ told them, " Ye are of your
father the devil." (John 8:44) Here He says, " You're the synagogue of Satan." Same message. Different group.

Yet despite this attack upon the church, Christ promises to
make these unbelievers bow down before them and acknowl-
edge their true relationship to God. Paul discovered that, " a
great and effectual door is open unto me AND THERE ARE
MANY ADVERSARIES." (1 Cor 16:9) OPPORTUNITIES
AND OBSTACLES. The Chinese word for CRISIS is a

combination of symbols for " danger," plus " opportunity." That's the way it is in God's kingdom. Opportunity usually comes in the face of crisis and danger.

(2) THE FUTURE WAS PARTICULARLY GRIM:

" Because thou hast kept .... earth." (3:10) The IMMEDI- ATE reference here would be to the official Roman persecutions that would come at any time. The storm might break upon this little church at any time. Surely, this is not a time for evangelism. Was this not a time for consolidation rather than advance ? But Christ had set before them " An open door," and they were to go through it. The IMMEDIATE REFERENCE IS TO LOCAL PERSECUTION, but the ULTIMATE REFERENCE is to UNIVERSAL TRIBULATION.

There is coming a time of worldwide upheaval the like of which has never been known in human history. The Bible calls this period, The day of the Lord: (Joel 2:1) The Indignation: (Is 26:20) The time of Jacob's trouble: (Jer 30:7) The seventieth week: (Dan 9:24-27) The great day of His wrath: (Rev 6:17) The Tribulation: (Matt 24:21 29)

The question is often asked: " Will the church go through the tribulation?" Are we looking for TRIBULATION or TRANSLATION? Are we looking for ANTICHRIST or JESUS CHRIST? In this connection chapter 3 verse 10 is interesting. The Greek phrase translated " keep from," does not mean " to preserve through something." Rather it means " To preserve outside the sphere of something." The Risen Lord is saying that He will PROTECT the Church by keeping them away from the very time when the wrath of God falls on the earth. In fact as (3:11) reminds us, the Lord will remove us from the earth before this period begins.

(d) AN OPEN DOOR IS PROJECTED BY THE BOOK:

" Prophetically, (1:3) the Philadelphia church represents the period from 1700-1900. It suggests the era of revival and missions. The great champions of this period were Jonathan Edwards, (1703-1758) one of America's greatest preachers and theologians. John Wesley, (1703-1791) the founder of the Methodist Church and one of England's greatest sons. George Whitefield, (1714-1770) William Carey, (1761-1834) David Livingstone, (1813-1873) D.L.Moody, (1837-1899) George Mueller, (1805-1898) and C.H.Spurgeon (1834-1892). " It was during this era that God brought the church back to Himself and thrust it forth to reach a lost world. Spirit filled servants of Christ went forth through the countries like firebrands of the Lord calling upon sinners to repent and saints to awaken. This was REVIVAL in the church and for this church the Risen Lord has nothing but praise.

(2) THE AUTHORITY THAT LAY BEHIND THEM

In (3:7) the Risen Lord says, " These things saith he that is holy, he that is true, he that hath the key of David, he that openeth, and no man shutteth, and shutteth, and no man openeth." In this self-description the Lord Jesus does something unique. This is the only church to whom Christ identifies Himself in a way not previously revealed in John's vision of (ch 1) This is because the vision of Christ was predominantly a vision of judgment. But as Christ speaks to this church, He has no complaint or criticism. Only commendation. So, an encouraging picture of Christ is revealed here instead. Behind this little fellowship was all the AUTHORITY OF THE RISEN LORD.

(a) THE RISEN LORD IS GOD:

" He that is Holy." (3:7) This is tantamount to declaring that He is God which of course He is. " The Holy One," is a title which Jehovah gave Himself in the Old Testament. (Is 40:25) So that the Lord Jesus is ONE with the God of the Old Testament. The concept of holiness comes from a Semitic root meaning, "to cut." To be holy is to be a cut above. Separate. Set apart.

Everything about the Lord Jesus is HOLY. He was HOLY at His BIRTH: " That holy thing .... the Son of God." (Lk 1:35) HOLY in His LIFE: " The Holy One of God." (Mk 1:24) HOLY at His DEATH: " Neither wilt Thou suffer Thine Holy One to see corruption." (Acts 2:27) HOLY in His Present PRIESTLY Office: " For such an high priest became us, who is Holy." (Heb 7:26) Majestic in His glory. Radiant in His splendour. Nothing can be compared to Him. He is the incomparable Christ.

(b) THE RISEN LORD IS GENUINE:

" He that is true." (3:7) That is genuine. (alethinos) It means He is authentic or genuine. Jesus Christ is no cheap imitation. No counterfeit Christ. No mimic Messiah. He is the real God who is true to His Word. He can be completely trusted because He is genuine Deity. He is not an imitation idol, but the authentic Almighty of heaven and earth.

(c) THE RISEN LORD IS GREAT:

He is Sovereign: " He that hath the key of David .... " (3:8) That means He is the Keeper of the Keys who alone opens and shuts the door leading to God's blessings. Christ has the,

(1) AUTHORITY TO REMIT SIN:

The scribes and Pharisees did not think so but the Lord said, " Son thy sins be forgiven thee." (Mk 2:5)

(2) AUTHORITY TO ADMIT SAINTS:

" He that hath the key of David." (3:8) The Scripture referred to here is (Is 22:22) King Hezekiah was king over the Davidic Kingdom and was served by a man called Eliakim as the royal treasurer. Eliakim was the guardian of the king's treasures. He alone possessed the keys to open the royal treasure vault. He controlled all access to the king's vast treasures. In just the same way the Lord Jesus has been handed the keys of heavens treasury by God the Father. These keys open the doors leading into the riches of God. Through Christ we have access into the Presence of God, the Riches of God, the Resources of God. Why would the Lord Jesus reveal Himself THIS way to THIS church? Because they had LITTLE strength and FEW resources. We need to be reminded that any church's strength does not lie in ITS SIZE but in ITS GOD.

(3) AUTHORITY TO PERMIT SERVICE:

" He that openeth .... " (3:8) Now the MESSENGERS of the Church need to hear this. So many preachers are prepared to " pull wires," " slap backs," " make the right contacts." We must spend less time recommending ourselves to others and more time showing ourselves approved to God, the Lord of the Open Door, who would open doors no man can shut. The MEMBERS of the Church need to hear this. If Christ is the "One who opens ...." then don't you BARGE your way through doors that are still closed. Be patient and wait until Christ takes out the KEY and opens the Door for you, for He is still in CONTROL.

(3) THE SECURITY THAT LAY BEYOND THEM

Christ says in (3:11) " Behold I come quickly .... " This is the Christian's hope. The Coming of the Lord, but the Risen Lord gives a warning. " Hold that fast which thou hast, that no man take thy crown." (3:10) It is not that " No man take thy salvation," that's eternally secure. I cannot lose my salvation but if I am not a faithful servant I can lose my crown.

(a) THE LORD WILL MAKE THE OVERCOMER:

What ? A pillar. You who have little strength. Where? "In the temple of my God." (3:12) You who were persecuted by the synagogue of Satan. Could anything be more appropriate? Philadelphia, was set on a fault line near the epicentre of the massive earthquake of AD 17. The slighest tremor in that city sent the citizens scurrying out of town. But in heaven, "they shall go out no more," (3:12) but will stand as pillars. Secure. Immoveable. Stable and Safe.

(b) THE LORD WILL MARK THE OVERCOMER:

Christ promises, " And I will write upon Him the name of My God." (3:12) In that day writing your name on something was a mark of ownership. A master would write his name upon his servants and that meant that the servant belonged to Him. We are His forever. Christ adds, " I will write upon him the name of the city." (3:12) Overcomers will receive all the rights of citizenship in the new Jerusalem. (Rev 21-22) Finally, Christ promises, " I will write upon him My new name." This symbolises the full revelation of His Divine Person. There are mysteries of beauty: of brilliance, and of blessing in Jesus not yet revealed to a wondering universe.

What the Queen of Sheba said to Solomon we will say to the Lord, " Behold the half was not told me." (1 Kings 10:7) For " eye hath not seen, nor ear heard, neither hath entered into the heart of man the things which God hath prepared for them that love Him." (1 Cor 2:9)

On May 31st 1792 William Carey preached his famous message in Nottingham, England. His text was (Is 54:2) "Enlarge the place of thy tent, and let them stretch forth the curtains of thine habitations: spare not, lengthen thy cords, and strengthen thy stakes." He packed his message into two great headings, "EXPECT GREAT THINGS FROM GOD ATTEMPT GREAT THINGS FOR GOD." Carey said, "The

Divine way out of failure and disgrace is a WIDER VISION and BOLDER PROGRAMME." He pleaded for action. His message so touched the hearts of those listening that a Missionary Society was formed which awoke the church from the lethargy of a thousand years. William Carey became its first missionary.

Philadelphia was " The Gateway to the East." The Risen Lord said, " I have set before thee an open door." (3:8)

Chapter Nine

It Makes God Sick

---------------------❖---------------------

Imagine a doctor being lukewarm about your disease. You feel sick so you drag yourself off to his surgery. He feels your pulse: takes your temperature and says good-bye. You say, "Well just a minute, whats wrong with me Doctor?" He looks up from the papers on his desk and says "What's wrong with you? Oh, theres nothing to worry about. You've a bad case of bubonic plague." You look at him in astonishment and say, "But aren't you going to give me an injection or put me in the hospital? People don't just walk around with bubonic plague do they? It's catching, isn't it? What about my family? What about all those people in your waiting room? What about ME? People die of bubonic plague, don't they?"

The Doctor just looks at you mildly and says, "That's all right my friend. You have to die sometime. It might just as well be bubonic plague as cancer or a coronary. Diseases don't interest me too much. Now, if you needed surgery, well that's more my line." Imagine a Doctor being lukewarm about disease. Imagine a church being lukewarm about Christ.

It makes as much sense. Yet such was the church at Laodicea. Now on the outside, this church looked eminently successful. Giving was up. Attendance was up. Activities were up. But Christ saw with X-ray vision into the heart and soul of this church. With divine omniscience, He got a completely different reading. Here's what He saw: unveiled before His eyes was a church that was neither hot nor cold. They were something in between .... lukewarm. And it is lukewarmness that MAKES CHRIST SICK.

In this letter, Christ addresses the sin of lukewarmness. This is a serious call to spiritual fervency, heart devotion, and holy zeal. Here is a solemn command to be ON FIRE for Christ, not lukewarm. This lukewarm church was situated in a very important city. It had been founded by Antiochus the Second and named after his wife. Laodicea was a very common name for women.

(1) COMMERCIALLY LAODICEA WAS FLOURISHING: That was due to two important factors.

(a) ITS POSITION WAS INFLUENTIAL: Strategically located, Laodicea occupied a critical juncture on the major roadway that ran from Ephesus in the west, to Phrygia in the east. Situated in the fertile Lycus Valley, it formed a tri-city combination with Hierapolis, six miles to the North and Colossae, ten miles east. Yet, it was definitely the hub, the judicial seat of the district. When a great earthquake in 60 AD levelled this and other surrounding cities, Laodicea refused government aid to rebuild, boasting that it had " need of nothing."

(b) ITS PEOPLE WERE INFLUENTIAL: It was to the banks of Laodicea that merchants and businessmen from all around came for financing their business abroad. Moreover, this city contained a large number of Jews who added to its wealth and prestige.

(2) MEDICALLY LAODICEA WAS FAMOUS: It was the seat of a famous medical centre, boasting a leading school of medicine. A well-known eyeslave that helped cure eye diseases (tephra phrygia) was developed by the physicians here. No doubt Christ has this in mind when He counsels the church, " Anoint thine eyes with eye salve .... " (3:18)

(3) AGRICULTURALLY LAODICEA WAS FRUITFUL: The surrounding countryside was famous for a certain black woollen sheep and this black wool would become woven into expensive garments. Consequently, they were a fashion conscious town with the latest styles. In the face of that the Lord says, " Buy white raiment that thou mayest be clothed." (3:18)

(4) SPIRITUALLY LAODICEA WAS FALLING: The first converts in this city probably came to Christ through the ministries of Paul and Epaphras. (Acts 19:8-10 Col 4:12-13) But however they may have prospered in those early days the church had now fallen on bad times. Consequently, the Risen Lord sends this church the sternest of the seven letters. Concerning the church at Philadelphia Christ had nothing BAD to say, concerning the church at Laodicea Christ had nothing GOOD to say. How searching this must be, for Prophetically speaking (1:3) there is brought before us THE CHURCH OF TODAY. Our own age.

This Laodicean period is characterised by the phenomenon of people dictating what will be taught rather than submitting to the authority of the Word of God. The name, " Laodicea," means " the judgment of the people," or to put it loosely, " the people's rights." Today, instead of people submitting themselves to the judgment of the Word of God, we have people submitting the Word of God to their own judgment. This is the age of COMPROMISE within the church. The church of the 20th century is fast becoming a lukewarm church, a nauseating church in the eyes of the Lord. Once the church exhibited a burning desire to evangelise the world, to reach the lost. Today, that desire has cooled in many churches.

The church in the 20th century is drifting away from Biblical truth. Once it was unheard of that professing Christians would suggest that the killing of unborn babies should be condoned, or that practicing homosexuals should be ordained to the ministry. Yet these things are taking place today at an accelerating rate. Truly, THIS IS the age of Laodicea, for which Christ has nothing but blame.

(1) THE CONDITION OF THIS CHURCH

What this church thought of itself was one thing, what Christ thought of this church was another thing. There is a big difference in (3:17) between " thou sayest," and " thou art." We can fool some of the people some of the time, but we can never fool Him any of the time.

(a) WHAT THE RISEN LORD REMARKS:

" I know thy works, that thou art neither cold nor hot, I would thou wert cold or hot. So then because thou art lukewarm, and neither cold nor hot, I will spue thee out of my mouth." (3:15-16) The Greek words here are striking and we are left in doubt about their meaning. " Cold," means icy cold and " Hot," (zestos) means boiling hot, but the word for " lukewarm," means " tepid," (chiliaros) and things which are lukewarm and tepid have a nauseating effect. The city of Laodicea was a thriving and prosperous city but it had one drawback and that was its water supply. Their drinking water had to be brought in from nearby towns to meet their needs in Laodicea.

There were two outside sources for their water .... Hierapolis and Colossae. An aqueduct brought some of their water six or seven miles from Colossae. This water was cold and good for drinking. Conversely, Hierapolis was famous for its hot underground springs. But there was just one problem. By the time the hot water of Hierapolis was brought to Laodicea, it had cooled off along the way. It was lukewarm and had lost its warm temperature. Likewise, by the time the cool water came from Colossae, the same change occurred. No longer cool and refreshing, it was insipidly lukewarm.

Now the same was spiritually true in the church. The Risen Lord says, " Thou art lukewarm." (3:16) To be lukewarm means to be half and half. Half cold, half hot. Blow cold, blow hot. Such a person is half-hearted toward Christ. A fence-strad-dler. Not wanting to commit one way or another. One foot in the world, one foot in the church. Someone with no zeal: no fire: no passion: and no heat.

(b) WHAT THE RISEN LORD REQUESTS:

" I would thou wert cold or hot." (3:15) Why does Christ say this ? Because the negative effect of a lukewarm Christian upon unbelievers is devastating. A lukewarm believer is the worst advertisement for Christianity. When a lost sinner sees the lukewarm Christian who is worldly, he reasons, " Why do I even need to be saved ? If this is what being a Christian is all about. I don't need Christianity. He's no different than me." The Risen Lord cannot tolerate this respectable nominal skin deep religiosity which is so widespread among us. He wants disciples who will go all the way. Indeed lukewarmness makes God sick, thus we notice:

(c) WHAT THE RISEN LORD RESOLVES:

" I will spue thee out of my mouth." (3:16) The word here for spew (emeo) means to " vomit, to throw up." If this condition continued without change Laodicea would not continue as a church. God is saying, " When you are indiffer-ent and lukewarm about Me, you make me sick to My stom-ach." God is not some kind of impassioned accountant in heaven, simply making marks in His divine ledger, running the universe in a cold, calculated way. He is someone with deep emotions, passionate zeal, and a loving heart. The Lord wants to have a personal, intimate relationship with us. But a lack of heart is utterly repugnant to Him. Christ says, " Get off the fence. Come out and out for Me. Or be out and out against Me. Just don't be indifferent. Get hot, get cold, or get out. Lukewarmness makes Me sick to my stomach."

(d) WHAT THE RISEN LORD REVEALS:

What is the cause of this indifference toward God ? Why were they lukewarm ? Christ exposes the problem when He says, " Because thou sayest, I am rich and increased with goods, and have need of nothing." (3:17) They were plagued with worldliness: materialism, and a smug self-sufficiency. Here were people absorbed with the things of this world. Climbing the social ladder. Advancing their career. Getting ahead in the world. The latest fashion style. Buying things. They lived for these pursuits. Pointedly the Risen Lord had to say to this shop-till-you-drop bunch, " and knowest not that thou art wretched .... " (3:17) " You think you're well attired, but you're naked ! You think you're getting ahead in the world, but you're broke ! You think you're something special, but you're wretched ! You may think you're happy but behind you're plastic smiles, you're miserable."

(2) THE CHOICE BEFORE THIS CHURCH

The Lord sets the choice before this church. Will it elect God's dealings in grace or His dealings in judgment ? Christ says, " I counsel thee .... and repent." (3:18-19) If this church was to be brought from LUKEWARMNESS to WHOLE-HEARTEDNESS,

(a) THE LORD'S PLAN MUST BE ACCEPTED:

Christ is speaking here to externally conscious, materialistic believers who are more excited about buying and shopping than about worshipping and praying. They are more passionate about temporal things than spiritual. To these

Christ says, " You need to do business with Me. You need what only I can give you. Instead of stockpiling material things, you need to acquire from me spiritual things." He tells them there must be a return:

(1) TO SPIRITUAL VALUES:

" I counsel thee to buy of me gold tried in the fire, that thou mayest be rich." (3:18) This speaks of spiritual riches. The church at Smyrna was MATERIALLY POOR but SPIRITU-ALLY RICH (2:9) Laodicea was MATERIALLY RICH but SPIRITUALLY POOR.

(2) TO SPIRITUAL VIRTUES:

" And white raiment that thou mayest be clothed." (3:18) The Laodiceans did not need the sleek black wool of their city, rather they needed to be clothed with the white garment that Paul speaks of when he says, " Put on therefore as the elect of God, holy and beloved, bowels of mercies, kindness, humble-ness of mind, meekness, longsuffering; Forbearing one another, and forgiving one another, if any man have a quarrel against any: even as Christ forgave you, so also do ye." (Col 3:12-14)

(3) TO SPIRITUAL VISION:

" And anoint thine eyes with eyesalve that thou mayest see." (3:18) This church was blind. They could not see reality.
They were living in a fool's paradise, proud of a church that was about to be rejected. The apostle Peter teaches that when a believer is not growing in the Lord his vision is af-fected. (2 Pet 1:5-9) " Diet," has a bearing on the condition of ones eyes, in a spiritual sense as well as a physical one. These people could not see themselves as they really were. Nor could they see the open doors of opportunity and they were blind to a lost world all around them. What did they need ? The illuminating ministry of the Holy Spirit.

(4) TO SPIRITUAL VIGOUR:

" Be zealous therefore and repent." (3:19) The word " zealous," means to be on fire. It pictures something reaching the boiling point. Christ is saying, " Turn your life around, and get on fire for me again. Rekindle your heart toward me before I have to discipline you."

(5) TO SPIRITUAL VICTORY:

" Be zealous therefore and repent." (3:19) The Risen Lord is saying, " Come, submit your life afresh to Me. Turn away from the things of the world. Repent of your preoccupation with your career: your house: your family: your recreations, or whatever else. Get refocused on Me. Repent and be zealous."

(b) THE LORD'S PERSON MUST BE RESPECTED:

The Risen Lord hammers home this PLAN by informing this fellowship of WHO HE IS. For only a startling self-disclosure of Himself could shake this church out of its spiritual lethargy. So here it is, " And unto the angel of the church of the Laodiceans," as if to say that the church at Laodicea was none of His: it was the church of the Laodiceans. " And unto the angel of the church of the Laodiceans write; These things saith the Amen, the faithful and true witness, the beginning of the creation of God." (3:14)

(1) HE IS THE TRUTHFUL ONE:

" The Amen." (3:14) The word denotes that which is true. When someone makes a statement we often say " Amen." We mean " that's the truth." Here Christ is saying, " I am the truth." (John 14:6) " Amen," implies certainty, veracity, and sincerity. Christ's words are absolute, unchangeable truth. This church needed to understand that Jesus Christ is the personification of truth. The ultimate reality. All other truth is measured by Him. His words are the divine standard. What He says is to be utterly relied upon. His words are to be embraced without reservation. No doubt Christ identifies Himself THIS WAY to THIS CHURCH because what He says will be a jolt to their system.

(2) HE IS THE FAITHFUL ONE:

" The faithful and true witness." (3:14) A witness is someone who testifies to what is true. Christ speaks the truth about what He has seen or heard. What He sees in the life of this church, He will faithfully testify to them. He will neither exaggerate nor surpress any of the truth. He is fully reliable to communicate the truth, the whole truth, and nothing but the truth.

(3) HE IS THE POWERFUL ONE:

" The beginning of the creation of God." (2:13) This does not mean that He is the first created being. Such an idea is theological heresy. Rather, this means that Jesus is the Creator (arche) of all creation. It was He who flung the stars into space: it was He who reared against the skyline of the world the mighty Himalayan range. " All things were made by Him." (John 1:3) Can we therefore ignore His plan ? Can we treat Christ with contempt ? He who is, " The Amen, the faithful and true witness, the beginning of the creation of God." (1:13)

Of this once famous church nothing now survives. He who has REMOVED THE CANDLESTICK at Ephesus, has SPUED Laodicea out of His mouth.

(3) THE CHALLENGE TO THIS CHURCH

" Behold I stand at the door and knock: if any man hear my voice , and open the door, I will come in to him, and will sup

with him, and he with me. To him that overcometh will I grant
to sit with me in my throne, even as I also overcame, and am
set down with my Father in his throne. He that hath an ear, let
him hear what the Spirit saith unto the churches. " (3:20-22)
We often use these verses to lead lost people to Christ, but the
basic interpretation is to the believer. The Lord Jesus, the Risen
Lord is outside the church at Laodicea pleading for individual's to give Him His rightful place. He challenges this church
with,

(a) HIS PERSON:

" Behold I stand .... " (3:20) He did not delegate a celestial
being to bring this message to Laodicea. He comes Himself.
The Bridegroom seeks His Bride, and all the communion that
should spring from her union with Him. In the Song of
Solomon the Bride said, " I sleep but my heart waketh," and
then she recognised the Bridegroom's voice, " It is the voice
of my beloved that knocketh saying, open to me, my love."
(Song of Sol 5:2)

(b) HIS PATIENCE:

" Behold I stand at the door and knock." (3:20) Or as the
sense of the verb has it, " I have taken my stand." He knocks
through circumstances and He calls through His Word. For
what is Christ appealing ? He is challenging us with,

(c) HIS PURPOSE:

" If any man .... and he with Me." (3:20) To us supper is
not a main meal. The Greek ate three meals in the day. Break-
fast (akratisma) was only a slice of bread dipped in wine.
Lunch (aristo) was seldom eaten at home. It was a quick
meal eaten in the city square or wherever a man happened to
be. But supper (deipon) was the main meal of the day. This
was the meal at which a man sat and talked. There was time

now, work was over. The Risen Lord wants to have unhurried, unlimited, unspeakable fellowship with us.

(d) HIS PROMISE:

" To him that overcometh .... (that is to the one who overcomes lukewarmness) will I grant .... His throne." (3:21) The Lord Jesus is looking forward here to the time of His Second Coming. When He returns, He will usher in His kingdom on earth, and at that time, our Lord will surround Himself with those who have been faithful to Him in this lifetime. All who have served Christ in this lifetime will be assigned places of special responsibility and will sit on the thrones to share in His millennial rule. One day the saints will rule and reign with Christ on the earth. (Matt 19:28 1 Cor 6:3 Rev 20:4)

Lukewarmness toward Christ is a gross sin against our Lord. Could it be that the greatest need of the church is to get FIRED UP for Christ ? The Challenge from the Risen Lord is a Personal one. " If any man." (3:20) " To him that overcometh." (3:21) In this Laodicean age the Risen Lord is taking up individual believers, for God can do great things through one man/woman totally given over to Him.

A church building once caught on fire. The entire neighbourhood ran down the street to see the church aflame. The fire was so intense that there was no hope of saving the buildings. Present among the bystanders was the town atheist. He was known for his unbelief and his cynical attacks on the church. As he stood there watching the church building burn, one of the members saw him and sarcastically said, "What are you doing here? I never thought I'd see YOU at church." The atheist replied, "You'll have to excuse me. But I've never seen a church on fire before."

And Finally ...

———————— ❖ ————————

Having studied the letter to each of the seven churches in Asia in some detail, we can conclude by looking at two items that were common to all of them.

Each letter begins with a challenging statement by the Master Judge. And ends with an encouraging thought from a loving Saviour.

Before pronouncing His verdict on the life and witness of each church the Saviour makes an emphatic declaration of His omniscience.

"I know thy works ..."

It can often be reassuring, when troubles and trials assail, to remember that the Saviour knows and cares.

We are reminded in Psalm 103 that, "He knoweth our frame; He remembereth that we are dust." (v 4)

And again Job comforts himself with the assurance, "He knoweth the way that I take: when he hath tried me, I shall come forth as gold" (ch. 23 v 10)

These thoughts are comforting. However, when we realise that He knows all of our works and acts it should make us careful how we live should it not?

Having begun each letter with an identical salutation, the Lord, in His summing up, ends each one with a promise.

"To him that overcometh ..."

Life may often appear tough. A battle and a struggle. We quite often seem to be swimming endlessly against the tide, while others meet us, happily riding the breakers to the shore.

Don't be discouraged.

"To him that overcometh," the Saviour makes a series of promises. "I will give ...", "I will grant ...", "I will make ...".

So let us keep going.

Serving. Witnessing. Preaching. Praying.

The Lord is coming soon.

And what's more ... His reward is with Him. (Rev 22 v 12)

Bibliography

1. Graham, R. J. (1967) Christ and His Churches. Saving Grace Union, Redhill, Surrey.
2. Havner, V. (1958) Messages on Revival. Fleming H. Revel Company, USA.
3. Ironside, H. (1930) Lectures on the Book of Revelation. Loizeaux Brothers, New York, USA.
4. Lahaye, T. (1973) Revelation Illustrated and Made Plain. Zondervan Publishing House, Grand Rapids, Michigan, USA.
5. Lawson, S. (1994) Final Call. Crossway Books, Wheaton, Illinois, USA.
6. Macarthur, J. (1973) Revelation. Certain Sound Publishing House, USA.
7. Macpherson, I (1973) News of the World to Come. Prophetic Witness Publishing House, Eastbourne, Sussex.
8. Pentecost, J. D. (1958) Things to Come. Zondervan Publishing House, Grand Rapids, Michigan, USA.
9. Pentecost, J. D. (1961) Prophecy for Today. Zondervan Publishing House, Grand Rapids, Michigan, USA.
10. Philips, J. (1974) Exploring Revelation. Moody Press, Chicago, USA.
11. Philips, J. (1983) Exploring the Future. Loizeaux Brothers, New Jersey, USA.
12. Rogers, A. (1995) Revelation. Volume One. Love Worth Finding Ministries, Memphis, Tennessee, USA.
13. Ryn, A.V. Notes on Revelation. Walterick Publishers, Kansas City, USA.
14. Ryrie, C. C. (1968) Revelation. Moody Press, Chicago, USA.
15. Scott, W. Exposition of the Revelation of Jesus Christ. Pickering and Inglis Ltd, London.
16. Stott, J. (1990) What Christ Thinks of the Churches. Word Publishing, Milton Keynes, England.
17. Strauss, L. The Book of Revelation. Loizeaux Brothers, New Jersey, USA.
18. Tatford, F. (1947) Prophecy's Last Word. Lowe and Brydone, London.

19.   Walvoord, J. F. (1966) The Revelation of Jesus Christ. Moody Press, Chicago, USA.

20.   Weaver, D. (1988) The Counsel of Christ to the Churches. Multiple Ministries, SC, USA.

21.   Wiersbe, W.W. (1989) The Bible Exposition Commentary. Victor Books, Wheaton, Illinois, USA.

22.   Willmington, H.L. (1988) Willmington's Guide to the Bible. Tyndale House Publishers Inc. Wheaton, Illinois, USA.

23.   Willmington, H.L. (1991) The King is Coming. Tyndale House Publishers Inc. Wheaton, Illinois, USA.